Target Vocabulary 3

Peter Watcyn-Jones

Illustrations by Neville Swaine

PENGUIN BOOKS

Pearson Education Limited
Edinburgh Gate, Harlow,
Essex CM20 2JE, England
and Associated Companies throughout the world.

First published by Penguin Books 1995
This edition published 2000
Third impression 2000

Printed in England by Clays Ltd, St Ives plc
Set in 11/16 pt Linotron Century Schoolbook

Published by Pearson Education Limited in association with
Penguin Books Ltd., both companies being subsidiaries of Pearson Plc

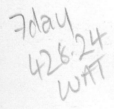

Contents

Section Three: Crime and punishment

59

Check 1 *(based on Sections 1–3)*

84

Section Four: Phrasal verbs

95

Section Five: Idioms 1

125

Section Six: Idioms 2   145

Introduction

Target Vocabulary 3 follows on from *Target Vocabulary 2* and is intended for intermediate/advanced students. It presents and practises approximately 1,200 key words which have been arranged into areas of vocabulary to facilitate learning. Altogether there are six main sections and each section has between 12 and 15 areas of vocabulary, closely linked to the main theme. Sections 1–3 concentrate on general vocabulary, while Sections 4–6 concentrate on phrasal verbs and idioms.

At the end of Section Three and Section Six there are mini tests called Check 1 and Check 2. These checks are for reinforcement and test the items in Sections 1–3, and 4–6 in a varied and interesting way.

Finally, to aid self-study, there is an answer key at the back of the book, plus a list of the key words used and the section(s) in which they appear.

In writing this book I have consulted a number of different dictionaries. The following can be warmly recommended:

Longman Language Activator (Longman)
Longman Dictionary of English Language and Culture (Longman)
Collins Cobuild Essential English Dictionary (Collins)
Oxford Advanced Learners Dictionary (Oxford University Press)
Collins Cobuild Dictionary of Phrasal Verbs (HarperCollins)
The Penguin Dictionary of English Idioms, Daphne M. Gulland and David G. Hinds-Howell (Penguin)
Oxford Pocket English Idioms, Jennifer Seidl and W. McMordie (Oxford University Press)

Section One: People

Types of people 1

Match the people 1–15 with the correct definitions a–o. Write your answers in the boxes on the next page.

f 1 An adolescent

j 2 An atheist

h 3 A benefactor

o 4 A bigot

a 5 A charlatan

l 6 A civilian

m 7 A genius

g 8 A hermit

b 9 An infant

n 10 An invigilator

d 11 A miser

k 12 A patriot

i 13 A penfriend

c 14 A sceptic

e 15 A tycoon

a falsely claims to have special skills or knowledge, especially in medicine.

b is a very young child or baby.

c does not readily believe claims or promises made by people.

d keeps count of every penny and really hates spending money.

e is a rich and powerful businessman or industrialist.

f is a young person who is no longer a child but not yet an adult.

g deliberately lives alone, away from other people and society.

h helps people by giving them money or other aid.

i is someone you write to but may never have met. He or she often lives abroad.

j doesn't believe in the existence of God.

k loves and supports his or her country and is willing to defend it.

l is anyone who is not a soldier or any other member of the armed forces.

3

m has very great ability and intelligence.

n supervises people taking an examination and makes sure they don't cheat.

o has strong and often unreasonable opinions and won't change them even when proved wrong.

1	2	3	4	5	6	7	8	9	10	11	12	13	14	15
f	j	h				m	g	b	n	d	k	i		e

Types of people 2

Match the people 1–15 with the correct definitions a–o. Write your answers in the boxes on the page opposite.

d 1 An adjudicator

k 2 An anarchist

f 3 An arbitrator

a 4 A beneficiary

l 5 A bystander

h 6 A conscript

j 7 A crank

m 8 A cynic

b 9 A degenerate

o 10 An expatriate

e 11 An imposter

a receives money or property from a will.

b behaves in a way that many people might find shocking or disgusting.

c is very proud of his or her country and believes it to be better than other countries.

d judges a competition.

e dishonestly pretends to be someone else in order to get something he or she wants.

f is called in to settle a dispute between two people or groups, usually at their request.

4

n 12 A juvenile

g 13 A loner

c 14 A nationalist

i 15 A scrounger

g prefers to spend time alone rather than in the company of other people.

h is made to serve in the armed forces of a country whether he or she wishes to or not.

i tries to get food and money without working for them.

j has peculiar ideas and behaves in a strange way.

k believes that all forms of government are oppressive and should be destroyed.

l is present when something happens and sees it, but does not take part in it.

m thinks people tend to act only in their own interests and are motivated by selfishness.

n is a child or young person who is not yet old enough to be regarded as an adult.

o is someone living in a country that is not their own.

1	2	3	4	5	6	7	8	9	10	11	12	13	14	15
d	k	f	a	e	h	p	m	b	o	c	n	g	c	i

Types of people 3

Read through the extracts below, then write the correct numbers 1–15 next to which type of person you think said the words. Choose from the following:

an agnostic	a picket	a spendthrift
a bully	a proprietor	a sponger
a castaway	a sadist	a squatter
a conscientious objector	a scapegoat	a teetotaller
a deserter	a snob	a veteran

1 'This shop is mine. I own it.'

2 'Do I save? You're joking! As soon as I get money I spend it. Don't ask me what on – it just goes.'

3 'A drink? No, thank you. I never touch alcohol.'

4 'I've been standing outside the factory gate for the past week. It's freezing and boring. I'll be glad when the strike's over.'

5 'Does God exist? Well, he might, but then on the other hand he might not. I just don't know.'

6 'You couldn't lend me some money, could you, Pete? You know how it is when you're out of work. And could I stay on at your place again?'

7 'I refuse to join the army. It's not right to fight and kill people.'

8 'I think it's so important to know the right people and shop in the right places, don't you? I really don't understand those who like to mix with the lower classes.'

9 'Yes, I'm proud to have served my country during the second World War. It's a long time ago now, but it still seems like yesterday.'

10 'Of course they're smaller and weaker than me. I wouldn't dare hit them otherwise!'

11 'Why shouldn't we live here? The building's been empty for six months and there's nowhere else for us to live except on the streets.'

12 'I couldn't stand being a soldier any longer, so I ran away. I just hope they don't catch me!'

13 'I can't explain why, but I just get a lot of pleasure out of hurting people and making them suffer.'

14 'It's now two weeks since the ship sank. Two whole weeks since I've been on this island. Will I ever be rescued, I wonder?'

15 'It wasn't really my fault, but they needed to blame someone for the mess. So, as I was chairman of the committee, they chose me.'

Follow up

Fill in the missing words in the following sentences. They are to be found in the previous three exercises.

1 Albert Einstein is probably the greatest _____ of the 20th century.

2 'Are you the _____ of this shop?'
   'No, I just work here. You want Mr Hearne.'

3 It was the first time she had acted as an _____ in a talent competition and found it quite difficult to judge the winner.

4 He's always asking for money and living off others. He's such a _____!

5 She's a _____ and prefers to spend time on her own rather than with others.

6 He claimed he was a doctor, but it turned out he was a complete _____ and had no medical qualifications whatsoever.

7 'Would you like a drink?'
   'No, thank you, I never touch alcohol. I'm a _____.'

8 Some anonymous _____ has just donated £10,000 to our Help the Homeless appeal.

9 During the strike nearly 200 _____ stood outside the factory gates trying to persuade people not to go to work.

10 No, I don't believe in flying saucers. I'm a _____ *sceptic* by nature and until I see one with my own eyes I won't believe they exist.

11 She's a _____. I've never heard such peculiar ideas and theories in my life.

12 I've got one _____ in Italy and another in Australia. I hope to meet them one day, but until then I'll just carry on writing letters.

13 He was a strong _____ and believed that Scotland should break away from the United Kingdom and have its own government and monarch.

14 It's not difficult to understand why homeless people become _____ when you see how many empty houses there are in our towns and cities.

15 In most wars, thousands of innocent _____ *civilians* usually get killed.

Idioms to describe people

Match the people 1–15 with the correct definitions a–o. Write your answers in the boxes on the page opposite.

1 A big shot

2 A blackleg

3 A busybody

4 A chatterbox

5 A daredevil

6 A dark horse

7 A gatecrasher

8 A grass widow

9 A guinea pig

a has a lot more capabilities than he or she shows or that people are aware of.

b is a failure or weak in some way and has to be helped by others.

c is usually expected to lose in a competition with someone else.

d always wants to know about other people's private lives.

e is a wife who is alone because her husband is temporarily away.

8

10 A lame duck

11 A pain in the neck

12 A road hog

13 An underdog

14 A wet blanket

15 A whizz kid

f   is a very selfish and careless driver.

g   is a real nuisance and most people can't stand him or her.

h   is someone who spoils the atmosphere or prevents others from enjoying themselves by being very boring and negative about everything.

i   can't stop talking.

j   is someone with lots of modern ideas, energy and enthusiasm and who achieves a lot while still young.

k   is a very important or influential person.

l   is used as a subject in medical or other experiments.

m   loves taking dangerous risks.

n   carries on working when his or her fellow-workers are on strike.

o   turns up at parties without being invited to them.

1	2	3	4	5	6	7	8	9	10	11	12	13	14	15
K			T	I										

Describing people: Character and personality 1

Match the following adjectives 1–20 with the correct meanings a–t to form complete sentences. Write your answers in the boxes on the page opposite.

People who are:

1 absent-minded f
2 adventurous l
3 amusing p
4 bashful t
5 boastful a
6 bright i
7 calm n
8 cheeky c
9 conceited r
10 confident g
11 creative s
12 domineering d
13 down-to-earth f
14 emotional b
15 enthusiastic k
16 gullible h
17 hospitable m
18 impatient j
19 malicious e
20 narrow-minded o

a like to say how good they are at something.

b have strong feelings and are easily moved by things.

c are rude and disrespectful, especially towards people like parents and teachers.

d are always trying to control others without worrying or caring about how they feel.

e deliberately try to hurt or harm others.

f are very forgetful because they are too busy thinking about other things.

g are sure of themselves and their abilities.

h are easily tricked and tend to believe everything they are told.

i are very clever and learn things quickly.

j hate having to wait for things and are not very tolerant of other people's weaknesses, etc.

k are very interested and excited about something and this shows in the way they talk or behave.

l are daring and always ready to take risks.

m are always friendly and welcoming towards guests.

n don't get excited or nervous about things.

o find it hard to accept or understand new or different ideas.

p are very funny and make you laugh.

q are very practical and honest.

r have a very high opinion of themselves.

s find it easy to produce new and original ideas and things.

t are shy and feel uncomfortable in social situations.

1	2	3	4	5	6	7	8	9	10	11	12	13	14	15	16	17	18	19	20

Describing people: Character and personality 2

Match the following adjectives 1–20 with the correct meanings a–t to form complete sentences. Write your answers in the boxes on page 13.

People who are:

1 aggressive g

2 articulate i

3 broad-minded n

4 charismatic

5 competitive d

a are usually very nervous and are easily upset or excited.

b are usually sure of their own ability to do things.

c are polite people.

d hate to lose at anything.

6 considerate †

7 courageous o

8 highly-strung a

9 humble q

10 modest e

11 obstinate m

12 pompous p

13 rash i

14 self-centred k

15 self-confident b

16 sensible r

17 strong-willed f

18 versatile l

19 well-mannered

20 witty h

e   tend to hide their abilities or have a lower opinion of themselves than is deserved.

f   know what they want and usually get it.

g   are always ready to quarrel or attack.

h   have quick minds and can express things in a clever and amusing way.

i   are very impulsive and don't think enough about the consequences of their actions.

j   are able to express clearly and effectively their thoughts and feelings.

k   are very selfish and only interested in themselves.

l   have lots of different skills and abilities and can easily change from one kind of activity to another.

m   refuse to change their opinion or behaviour in spite of attempts to persuade them to do something else or to see another point of view.

n   are very tolerant of other people's opinions even if very different from their own.

o   are very brave and not afraid to do dangerous things.

p   take themselves rather too seriously and think they are very important.

q   have a very low opinion of themselves and a high opinion of others.

r   are people with a lot of common sense.

s have very strong personal charm and the power to attract others.

t are very aware of the wishes, needs or feelings of others.

1	2	3	4	5	6	7	8	9	10	11	12	13	14	15	16	17	18	19	20

Describing people: Character and personality 3

Match the following adjectives 1–20 with the correct meanings a–t to form complete sentences. Write your answers in the boxes at the bottom of the next page.

People who are:

1 cocky

2 conscientious

3 impressionable

4 level-headed

5 loyal

6 neurotic

7 open

8 practical

9 prejudiced

10 pushy

11 ruthless

12 secretive

13 shrewd

a are always willing to discuss things honestly.

b are very good at making practical judgements, especially when they are to their own advantage.

c are easily moved to pity and very quick to forgive.

d say one thing to one person, then the opposite thing at another time to someone else.

e often have unfair or unreasonable opinions about people and things – usually because of fear or distrust of ideas or people different from themselves.

f often try to harm or annoy others, especially in some small way.

13

14 single-minded r

15 smug j

16 soft-hearted c

17 spiteful f

18 strict n

19 talented h

20 two-faced d

g are easily influenced by other people and often too ready to admire them.

h have a special natural ability or skill, e.g. in music or painting.

i never desert you in a crisis and are always ready to give you their support.

j are too pleased with themselves and their qualities, position, etc.

k are very self-confident, but in an unpleasant way.

l are always demanding things from others and trying to get what they want.

m are unreasonably anxious or sensitive.

n like to be obeyed and are strong believers in discipline.

o are careful to do any work well.

p are usually without remorse, pity or forgiveness.

q are calm and sensible when making judgements.

r don't let anything get in the way of their main aim in life.

s like to keep their thoughts and intentions hidden from others.

t are clever at doing things and dealing with difficulties.

1	2	3	4	5	6	7	8	9	10	11	12	13	14	15	16	17	18	19	20

Describing people: Character and personality 4

Read through the statements below, then decide the character or personality of the people who said them. Write the correct numbers 1–16 next to the adjectives below.

Find someone who is:

bigoted 7	determined 16	indecisive 5	thrifty 11
blunt 6	extravagant	naïve 15	understanding 3
callous 4	fussy 12	possessive 2	unreliable 2
cynical 14	illiterate 8	superstitious 9	weak-willed 16

1 'I've just spent £600 on David's birthday party. Well, you're only seven once in your life, aren't you?'

2 'I don't really like my wife going out on her own or with her friends. I prefer her to spend all her time with me.'

3 'Of course you can have the afternoon off to visit your wife in hospital. And take tomorrow off too, if you need to. Don't worry, we'll manage.'

4 'No, I don't like your dress, actually. It makes you look fat.'

5 'Shall I buy the blue curtains or the red ones? The blue ones are nice but the red ones will go better with the wallpaper. On the other hand, David prefers blue. Oh, I don't know what to get.'

6 'No, I'd better not have a chocolate biscuit, thanks, I'm on a diet. But they do look nice, don't they? Oh, all right then, just one.'

7 'All Conservatives are rich, upper class snobs. I've got no time for any of them, especially the Prime Minister. Working-class people will always be poor with a Conservative government.'

8 'I'm sorry, you'll have to help me fill in this form. I can't read or write.'

9 'I never walk under ladders. It's bad luck!'

10 'So some children have died. So what? This is war, not a Christmas Party.'

11 'I'm always very careful with money. I never buy anything I don't need, for example.'

12 'Don't forget to cut the fat off the bacon before you fry it and remember to use margarine not butter. And also make sure that the eggs are soft this time – you know hard-boiled eggs don't agree with me.'

13 'I know it's the third time now I haven't turned up for a match, but I overslept. It wasn't really my fault.'

14 'He's only doing it for the publicity. I don't believe for one minute he's really interested in helping mentally-handicapped people.'

15 'But I believed him when he said he was a famous fashion photographer and could make me into a top model.'

16 'I'm going to get a book published one day. I'm just not going to give up until I do.'

Follow-up: How do you rate yourself?

Look at the following statements and think of how they apply to you. Try to rate yourself on a scale of 1–10, where 1 is the lowest and 10 the highest. (Put a circle around the number.)

1 I am aggressive	1	2	3	4	5	6	7	8	9	10
2 I am competitive	1	2	3	4	5	6	7	8	9	10
3 I am creative	1	2	3	4	5	6	7	8	9	10
4 I am cynical	1	2	3	4	5	6	7	8	9	10
5 I am emotional	1	2	3	4	5	6	7	8	9	10
6 I am gullible	1	2	3	4	5	6	7	8	9	10
7 I am impatient	1	2	3	4	5	6	7	8	9	10
8 I am obstinate	1	2	3	4	5	6	7	8	9	10
9 I am practical	1	2	3	4	5	6	7	8	9	10
10 I am self-confident	1	2	3	4	5	6	7	8	9	10
11 I am strong-willed	1	2	3	4	5	6	7	8	9	10
12 I am superstitious	1	2	3	4	5	6	7	8	9	10

13 I am talented	1 2 3 4 5 6 7 8 9 10
14 I am two-faced	1 2 3 4 5 6 7 8 9 10
15 I am witty	1 2 3 4 5 6 7 8 9 10

When you have finished, work with a partner. Take it in turns to tell each other four or five things you have written about yourselves.

Describing people: Moods and feelings 1

Match the adjectives 1–16 with the correct meanings a–p to form complete sentences. Write your answers in the boxes at the bottom of the next page.

People who are/feel:

1 amazed

2 anxious

3 bad-tempered

4 cheerful

5 contented

6 disillusioned

7 fed up

8 heartbroken

9 humiliated

10 irritable

11 miserable

12 nostalgic

13 scared

14 sceptical

15 sentimental

16 thrilled

a feel bitter and disappointed because they've lost their belief that someone is good or that an idea or plan is right.

b are frightened.

c feel very ashamed and upset, especially because they've been made to look weak or stupid.

d are very unhappy.

e are very easily affected by emotions such as sympathy, love or sadness.

f are happy and in good spirits.

g are easily annoyed and tend to get angry at small things, often because they already feel bad-tempered about something.

h like remembering happy events or experiences from the past, often because they are not so happy with their lives now.

7 i are unhappy and feel dissatisfied or bored.

1 j are so surprised that they find it hard to believe what has happened.

k don't really believe what other people tell them.

l get angry very easily and behave in a very angry and unfriendly way.

m are extremely pleased, happy and excited. It could be because they've been told some good news or are going to do something that they've always wanted to.

n are feeling very worried and nervous about something that may or may not have happened.

o are very sad because they have been upset or deeply hurt by something that has happened.

p are satisfied and quite happy with their lives.

1	2	3	4	5	6	7	8	9	10	11	12	13	14	15	16

Describing people: Moods and feelings 2

Match the following adjectives 1–15 with the correct meanings a–o to form complete sentences. Write your answers in the boxes on the next page.

People who are/feel:

1 annoyed

2 apprehensive

3 baffled

4 complacent

5 down

6 edgy

7 furious

8 homesick

9 light-headed

10 mixed-up

11 paranoid

12 petrified

13 resentful

14 speechless

15 touchy

a are feeling sad and depressed.

b find it hard to think clearly or move steadily. You can often feel like this after drinking alcohol.

c are nervous and can't seem to relax or behave in a calm way.

d are unable to say anything because they are angry, upset or shocked.

e are so frightened that they can't move.

f feel slightly angry.

g are confused and unable to decide what to do. This is often because of personal or emotional problems.

h are angry and bitter about something they think is unfair.

i are worried and nervous about the future or something they're going to do.

j are extremely angry.

k are too sensitive and are easily offended or annoyed.

l are completely unable to explain or understand something.

m are unhappy because they're away from home and missing their family, friends, etc.

n are constantly convinced that people hate them or that bad things will happen, even though this isn't true.

o are so pleased with their achievements or the situation they're in that they don't think there's any need to worry or make an effort.

1	2	3	4	5	6	7	8	9	10	11	12	13	14	15

Follow up

Fill in the missing words in the sentences below. They are to be found in the previous two exercises.

1 They were really _____ when their daughter told them she was expecting a baby. At last they would have their first grandchild.

2 She was _____ when she heard that someone else had been given the job she was after. I don't think I've ever seen her so angry before.

3 We were all _____ when she told us she was nearly seventy-three. She really didn't look a day over sixty.

4 My parents have a burglar alarm, locks on every window, large bolts on the doors, an Alsatian dog and security lights outside. They're _____ about being burgled, which is strange as they live next door to the police station.

5 When the mugger put a knife to her throat and asked her to hand over her money she was _____ and for a minute she thought she was going to die.

6 After so many years under Margaret Thatcher many people became _____ with politics in general and the Conservative Party in particular.

7 When his dog died the old man was _____. It had been his friend and faithful companion for over sixteen years and it felt as painful as losing a child.

8 When they first moved to France they were very _____. They missed Britain, their family, and their friends. They even missed complaining about the weather!

9 The police are _____ as to how the thieves managed to steal the painting from the gallery without the alarm going off.

10 Don't mention work tonight at dinner. John's become _____ about things like that since he lost his job.

11 Listening to old Beatles records always makes me feel _____ and wish I was still living in the '60s.

12 The young man felt _____ as he sat in the waiting-room before his interview. It was the first time he had ever applied for a job.

Jobs people do 1

Match the jobs 1–15 on the left with the correct definitions a–o. Write your answers in the boxes on page 23.

1 An ambassador

2 An auditor

3 An au pair

4 A bailiff

5 A bookie/bookmaker

6 A bouncer

7 A civil engineer

8 A civil servant

9 A frogman

10 A headhunter

a is someone you go to if you want to place a bet in a horse race or a dog race.

b works underwater and wears special rubber clothing and breathing equipment.

c owns or manages a pub.

d is usually a strong man who is employed to stand at the door of a club or restaurant. His job is to stop unwelcome people from coming in and to throw out anyone inside who is causing trouble.

11 An ombudsman *g*

12 A pawnbroker *o*

13 A publican *c*

14 A shop steward *i*

15 An underwriter *f*

e is a diplomat of the highest rank who lives in a foreign country and represents his or her own country's interests there.

f makes insurance contracts.

g is appointed by the government to receive and report on complaints made by ordinary people against the government or other public services.

h is usually a young girl from a foreign country who lives with a family in order to learn the language, in return for helping with the children and housework.

i is a trade union official who is elected by the other members in the factory or office where he or she works to represent them.

j plans buildings and the repair of roads, bridges, large public buildings, etc.

k is an accountant who officially examines the accounts of businesses.

l tries to attract talented people to a new job by offering them, for example, better pay or greater responsibility than they have in their present one.

m is a law officer who takes possession of people's goods or property when they owe money.

n works for a country's government department.

o lends people money in return for something they own, such as jewellery, fur coats, etc. He or she has the right to sell the item if the money is not paid back before a certain date.

1	2	3	4	5	6	7	8	9	10	11	12	13	14	15

Jobs people do 2

What jobs do the people below have? Write the correct numbers 1–10 next to the following words. (Six of the words will not be used.)

an archaeologist	a critic	a lumberjack
a baby-sitter	a disc jockey	a nanny
a bodyguard	an editor	a solicitor
a broker	a lifeguard	a surveyor
a busker	a locksmith	a taxidermist
a composer		

1 'I work for a newspaper. I'm the person in charge of it. I usually write the editorial too.'

2 'People usually come to me for legal advice. I also have to appear in court sometimes on behalf of my clients.'

3 'I risk my life every day protecting rich or important people. I get well-paid but most of the people I protect can afford it.'

4 'I work for a wonderful family in Kensington. Baby Emma and I get on really well, which is fortunate as we spend most of the day together. I think the people I live with and work for are very pleased with the way I'm looking after their daughter.'

5 'I suppose I have quite a pleasant job really. I spend most of my time at the theatre or cinema where, after seeing a new film or a play, I write a review about it for the newspaper I work for.'

6 'Women like being married to me because the older they get the more interested I become in them, they say. Seriously though, my job is all about looking at very old things – buildings, pots, tools, weapons, and so on. In fact, I'm off to Egypt next month

to examine a new tomb they've found there. I'm hoping it could be another Tutankhamen.'

7 'I spend most of my time playing my guitar in the street or at Underground stations. I think people quite like me because they throw a lot of money into my open guitar case.'

8 'I work at the local swimming pool and in the summer at the local beach. Its my job to rescue anyone in danger of drowning. So far I've saved about twenty people's lives.'

9 'People often come to me when their pet dog or cat has died. They can't bear to part with them, so I stuff and mount the animals so that they look almost alive and the owners can go on seeing them, talking to them, and so on.'

10 'Many of my clients are people buying a house. They want me to examine it to make sure the structure's all right, etc. I examine everything then give them a written report. There's usually something wrong with most houses, but so far I've only found three houses that I would definitely not recommend.'

Parts of the body

1 *How many of the following words do you know?* Work in pairs. Take it in turns to read out one of the words below. Your partner now tries to point to the appropriate part of his or her body. If correct, the word is crossed out.*

ankle	forehead	thigh
cheek	heel	throat
chest	jaw	thumb
chin	knee	tongue
elbow	neck	waist
eyebrow	shoulder	wrist
eyelash	stomach	

Were there any words you didn't know?

* These words appeared in *Target Vocabulary 1* (Penguin)

2 *Here are some new and more difficult words to describe parts of the body. Look at the drawings here and on page 26, then write the correct numbers 1–28 next to the following words.*

Adam's apple	eyelid	nostril
bags under the eyes	freckles	parting
crow's feet	lobe	scar
dimple	mole	temple
double chin	moustache	wrinkles

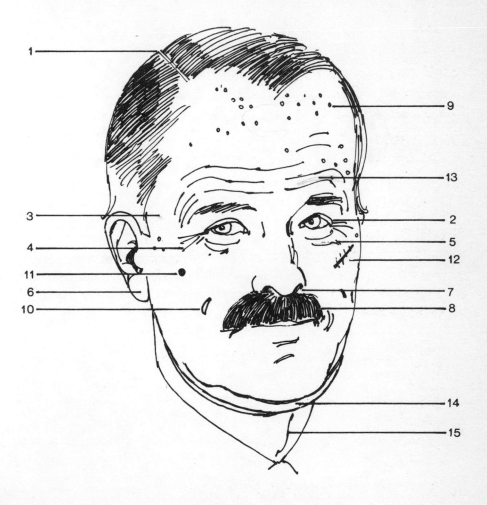

armpit 13   calf 18   instep 22   palm 27
back 24   fist 7   knuckle 8   pot belly 20
biceps 16   hip 26   navel 19   shin 21
bust 15

Parts of the body verbs

Here are twelve parts of the body that can also be used as verbs. Put them in the sentences 1–12 below. Use each verb once only and make any changes where necessary.

elbow	hand	nose	stomach
face	head	palm	thumb
foot	knuckle	shoulder	toe

1 The teacher told the pupil that she would really have to _____ down if she wanted to pass the exam.

2 I could never be a soldier and fight in a war. I just couldn't _____ the killing.

3 Since both his fiancée's parents were dead, his own parents offered to _____ the bill for the wedding.

4 Although some members of the party didn't agree with the new tax on books and magazines, they decided to _____ the line, rather than vote against their own party.

5 I tried to stop the shoplifter but she _____ me out of the way

6 If Mike tries to _____ off his old computer on you, just tell him you're looking for something more up-to-date.

7 The way she drives she's _____ for an accident.

8 As they had missed the last bus they decided to try to _____ a lift home.

9 After hiding from the police for three weeks, he finally decided to give himself up and _____ the music.

10 He had to sack his cleaner because he found her _____ about among his private letters and documents one morning.

11 She _____ me a cup of tea and told me to help myself to milk and sugar.

12 The Government is being asked to _____ the cost of tidying up after the recent floods.

In other words...

At the end of each section in this book you are going to learn some common and useful idioms. Try to learn them by heart as they will help you to read newspapers, magazines and understand everyday conversations.

(a) *Match the sentences 1–10 with a suitable idiom a–j. Write your answers in the boxes on the next page.*

1 He got up and made a speech without any preparation or notes.

2 He promised not to tell anyone about her brother being in prison.

3 'It was really cheap. I only paid £15 for it.'

4 He was very fond of his granddaughter.

5 He wanted to laugh, but managed to control himself.

6 He was really frightened.

7 'I asked him how his wife was. How was I to know she was dead?'

8 He made fun of the way the man spoke and looked.

9 'My brother lost his job last week for hitting a foreman.'

10 'It was a joke, David. He wasn't being serious.'

a He had a soft spot for her.

b He took the mickey out of him.

c He kept a straight face.

d He put his foot in it.

e He got the sack.

f He did it off the cuff.

g He was pulling your leg.

h He got it for a song.

i He was shaking like a leaf.

j He gave his word.

1	2	3	4	5	6	7	8	9	10

(b) *Now complete the following six dialogues with a suitable idiom.*
Choose from the above list and make any necessary changes.

1 A: How's the new job, Judy?

    B: Haven't you heard? I _____ last week.

2 A: That's a lovely desk. Was it expensive?

    B: No, I _____ because the owner was going abroad.
It only cost £30.

    A: That was a bargain!

3 A: What did you think of his speech?

    B: Wasn't it awful! I really don't know how I managed to
_____. I was dying to laugh.

    A: Yes, me too.

4 A: Carol's uncle really spoils her, doesn't he?

    B: Yes, he's always _____ his niece.

5 A: That was an excellent speech, Margaret. It must have taken
you ages to prepare.

    B: No, I didn't know they were going to ask me to say
anything. I _____.

6 A: _____ that you won't tell anyone about this.

    B: Don't worry, Peter, I won't say a thing. I promise.

Section Two: Health and illness

Inside the body

Look at the two drawings on these pages then write the correct numbers 1–20 next to the following words.

artery	intestines	pelvis/hip-bone	spine/
bladder	kidney	ribs	backbone
brain	kneecap	shin bone	vein
breastbone	liver	shoulder blade	vertebrae
collar bone	lung	skull	windpipe
heart			

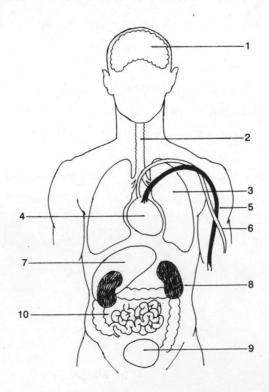

Internal organs

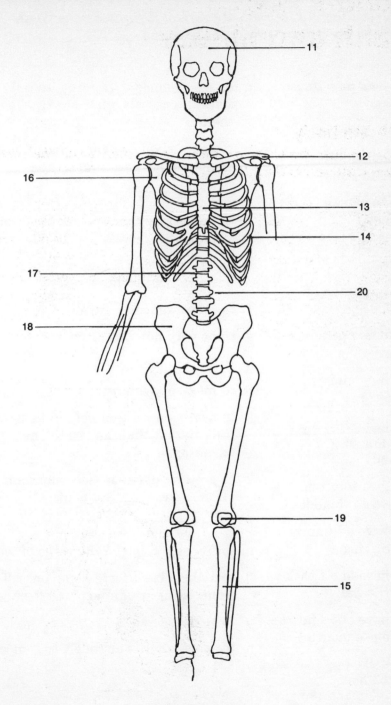

The skeleton

Parts of the body idioms

Match the idioms 1–16 with the correct definitions a–p. Write your answers in the boxes on the opposite page.

1 to be a pain in the neck

2 to be all ears

3 to be all fingers and thumbs

4 to be all skin and bones

5 to be down in the mouth

6 to be rushed off one's feet

7 to bite a person's head off

8 to bite one's tongue

9 to give someone a piece of one's mind

10 to give someone the cold shoulder

11 to have a lump in one's throat

12 to have one's back to the wall

13 to have one's heart in one's mouth

14 to make one's blood boil

a to scold someone severely; to tell someone angrily what one thinks of them

b to be in a bad or dangerous situation from which there is no escape

c to deliberately ignore someone

d to be so busy that one doesn't have time to stop or rest

e to be a pest and a nuisance; to be an irritating, annoying person

f to greet someone warmly

g to be very nervous or frightened

h to be very clumsy

i to make one angry

j to listen very attentively to news or information that may be to one's advantage

k to pretend not to notice something, often something that is illegal

l to be very thin

m to feel sad; to be on the verge of tears

n to make a big effort to stop oneself from saying what one really feels

o to be depressed

p to speak angrily or rudely to someone

15 to turn a blind eye
   to something

16 to welcome someone
   with open arms

1	2	3	4	5	6	7	8	9	10	11	12	13	14	15	16

Follow up

Rewrite the following sentences using a suitable idiom from the above list. To help you, a part of the body is given in brackets after each sentence.

1 The mother was on the verge of tears as she tried to talk about her dead son. *(throat)*

2 All right, all right! Calm down! There's no need to be so angry! *(head)*

3 He drove like a madman along the motorway and I was very frightened all the way to London. *(mouth)*

4 I hope she doesn't bring her kid brother this time – he was a real pest the last time he was here. *(neck)*

5 What have I done to Pamela? She's been completely ignoring me all morning. *(shoulder)*

6 Seeing young people carrying racist banners really makes me angry. *(blood)*

7 She needs to eat more – she's so thin. *(skin)*

8 She saw the girl taking sweets from the shop, but pretended she hadn't noticed her. *(eye)*

9 When she found out that he hadn't done what he had promised to do, she really told him what she thought of him. *(mind)*

10 You're looking depressed today, Terry. Come on, cheer up! *(mouth)*

Medical equipment, etc.

Look at the drawings on these pages and write the correct numbers 1–20 next to the following words.

adhesive tape	ointment	thermometer
bandage	pill/tablet	tweezers
capsule	plaster cast	walking frame
cotton wool	safety pin	walking stick
crutch	sling	wheelchair
hearing aid	stethoscope	X-ray
(hypodermic) needle	stretcher	

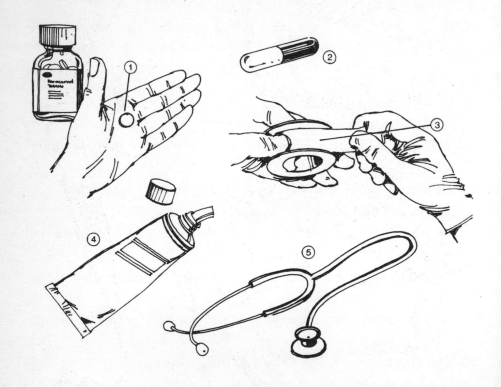

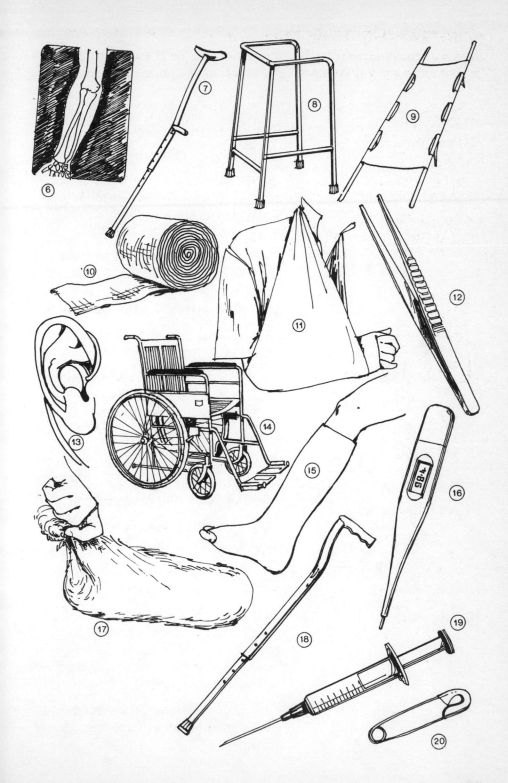

Who's who in medicine

Match the people below 1–20 with the correct definitions a–t. Write your answers in the boxes at the bottom of the page opposite.

1 A casualty

2 A chiropodist

3 A chiropractor

4 A consultant

5 A district nurse

6 A general
  practitioner (GP)

7 A home help

8 A matron

9 A midwife

10 A nurse

11 An optician

12 An osteopath

13 An out-patient

14 A pathologist

15 A paediatrician

16 A pharmacist

17 A physiotherapist

18 A psychiatrist

19 A specialist

20 A surgeon

a is a person, usually a woman, who has been trained to advise pregnant women and to help them when they are giving birth.

b is a person who treats illness and physical problems by moving and pressing muscles and bones.

c is a person who is trained to treat patients by giving them exercise or massage, often to help them walk again after an accident or operation.

d is a doctor whose job is to perform operations.

e is a person who has been injured or killed in an accident, a fire or a war.

f is a person who tests people's eyesight and provides glasses and contact lenses.

g is a doctor who examines a dead body to find out how the person died.

h is a doctor who treats people suffering from mental illnesses.

i is a person who is trained to treat and care for people's feet.

j is a doctor trained in general medicine who treats people in a certain local area for all kinds of illnesses. He or she is usually the first doctor people go to when they are ill.

k is a doctor who specializes in one area of medical treatment, e.g. an eye
____ .

l   is a person who is employed by the medical and social services to help people who are old or ill with their cleaning, cooking, shopping, etc.

3 m   is a person who treats diseases by feeling and pressing the bones, especially those of the back and neck.

n   is a person who is qualified to prepare and sell medicines.

o   is the woman in charge of the nurses in a hospital. Nowadays she is officially called a senior nursing officer.

p   is a high-ranking and very experienced hospital doctor who gives specialist advice in one particular area of medicine.

q   is a person who has to visit a hospital regularly for treatment while still living at home.

r   is a person who looks after patients in hospital.

s   is a nurse, employed by the local authority, who visits and treats people in their own homes.

t   is a doctor who specializes in treating sick children.

1	2	3	4	5	6	7	8	9	10	11	12	13	14	15	16	17	18	19	20
9	2	17	18		11														

What's wrong with them?

Look at the drawings below and write under each one what is wrong with the person. The following words should help you.

a bad cough	a temperature	hard of hearing
a black eye	blind	high blood-pressure
a migraine	break one's leg	pregnant
a nose-bleed	burn oneself	sea-sick
a rash	catch a cold	sprain one's ankle
a sore throat	crippled	to be stung
a stomach ache	faint	

1 She's _____

2 He's _____

3 He's _____

4 She's _____

5 He's _____

6 She's _____

7 He's _____

8 She's _____

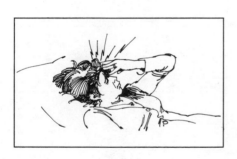

9 She's _____

10 He's _____

11 She's _____

12 He's _____

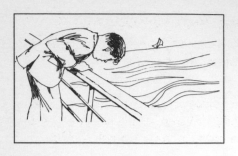

13 He's _____

14 She's _____

15 She's _____

16 He's _____

17 She's _____

18 He's _____

19 She's _____

20 He's _____

Common diseases, illnesses and conditions 1

Match the words 1–16 below with the correct definitions 1–16. Write your answers in the boxes at the bottom of page 42.

1 An allergy

2 Anaemia

3 Asthma

4 A chill

5 Concussion

6 A fever

7 Flu/influenza

8 Food poisoning

9 A heart attack

10 Indigestion

11 Insomnia

12 Measles

13 Nausea

14 A nervous breakdown

15 Rheumatism

16 A stroke

a is an infectious disease which is like a bad cold. When you have it you feel very weak and your muscles ache.

b is an infectious illness where you have a fever and small red spots on your face and body.

c is an illness that makes your joints or muscles stiff and painful.

d is a condition associated with many illnesses where you develop a high temperature.

e is a serious medical condition, sometimes fatal, in which your heart begins to beat irregularly or fails to pump your blood properly so that it causes a lot of pain.

f is a condition of being very sensitive to things such as food, animals, medicine, dust, etc., which often results in rashes or difficulty in breathing.

g is a sudden and severe illness which affects your brain and which can kill you or make you paralysed in one side of your body.

h is a mild illness which can give you a slight fever, a headache and your body might shake.

i is the feeling of wanting to be sick. The feeling that you think you are going to vomit.

j is an injury to the brain caused by a blow to your head. It is not normally long-lasting.

k is an illness where you suffer from deep depression, worry and tiredness. You often cry uncontrollably and find it almost impossible to do your normal work or activities.

l is an unhealthy condition in which you have too few red cells in your blood, which makes you look pale and feel tired.

m is a pain that you get in your stomach when you find it difficult to digest your food.

n is a painful stomach disorder caused by eating food which has gone bad.

o is a long-lasting chest disease which at times makes breathing very difficult.

p is the condition of being constantly unable to sleep.

1	2	3	4	5	6	7	8	9	10	11	12	13	14	15	16

Common diseases, illnesses and conditions 2

Match the words 1–16 below with the correct definitions a–p. Write your answers in the boxes at the bottom of the next page.

1 Amnesia

2 Anorexia

3 Cancer

4 Catarrh

5 A cold

6 A coma

7 Cramp

8 Diabetes

9 Dyslexia

10 Epilepsy

11 Hay fever

12 An inflammation

13 Malaria

14 Malnutrition

15 A miscarriage

16 Pneumonia

a is an illness similar to a cold, in which you sneeze a lot. People often get it in the summer because they are allergic to pollen from various plants.

b is losing a baby because it is born too early for it to live. It is usually because of illness, shock, etc.

c is a deep, unnatural sleep-like state, usually caused by illness or an injury, especially to the brain.

d is a problem with reading caused by difficulty in seeing the difference between the shapes of letters. It is also known as 'word-blindness'.

e is a serious disease which may cause death, in which the cells in your body increase rapidly and uncontrollably, producing abnormal growths.

f is a serious disease which affects your lungs and makes it difficult for you to breathe.

g is a mild, very common illness which makes you sneeze a lot and gives you a sore throat or a cough.

h is a painful swelling and soreness of part of the body, which is often red and hot to the touch.

i is the medical condition of not being able to remember anything. It is usually caused by damage to the brain after an accident, disease, etc.

j   is a common disease in hot countries. It is spread by mosquitoes and causes attacks of fever and shivering.

k   is a strong pain caused by the sudden tightening of a muscle. You often get it during or after violent exercise.

l   is a serious illness common mostly in young women. They lose the desire to eat because they feel they are unattractive because they are too fat, even when they are not.

m   is an illness of the brain which causes you to suddenly lose consciousness or to have fits.

n   is a disease in which there is too much sugar in the blood. If you suffer from it, you may have to inject insulin into your body every day. Without insulin, you may go into a coma and die.

o   is an inflammation of the nose and throat which, like having a cold, makes your nose feel blocked up.

p   is poor health caused by not eating enough food or by not eating enough of the right kinds of food.

1	2	3	4	5	6	7	8	9	10	11	12	13	14	15	16

Follow up

What illnesses, diseases or conditions are the following drawings illustrating? The answers are to be found in the previous two exercises.

Skin and body disorders

Look at the drawings below and write the correct numbers 1–10 next to the following words.

a blister	a bump	a mole	varicose veins
a boil	a corn	pimples	a wart
a bruise	a cut		

46

Group the words

Here are twenty words in alphabetical order. Write each word under the correct heading (10 words under each).

ambulance	emergency	lozenge	tranquillizer
anaesthetic	fracture	operation	unconscious
antibiotics	insulin	pain killer	vaccination
aspirin	kiss of life	patient	ward
cough mixture	laxative	sleeping tablet	X-ray

Medicine, medication and drugs

Hospitals and accidents

_____   _____

_____   _____

_____   _____

_____   _____

_____   _____

_____   _____

_____   _____

_____   _____

_____   _____

_____   _____

What is the difference between the following?

1   an antibiotic – an antiseptic
2   a sleeping tablet – a tranquillizer
3   a fracture – an X-ray
4   a vaccination – anaesthetic

At the doctor's

Fill in the missing words in the passage below. Choose from the following:

appointment	lung cancer	stethoscope
blood pressure	medicine	surgery
couch	prescription	symptoms
examination	pulse	temperature
GP	receptionist	waiting-room

Last week I phoned my (1) _____ to make an (2) _____ to see her, as I had been feeling a bit under the weather recently.

When I arrived at her (3) _____, there were only two other people in the (4) _____. I gave my name to the (5) _____ and sat down to await my turn. Fortunately, I didn't have to wait long.

The doctor asked me what was wrong, so I told her my (6) _____, namely that I had been feeling very tired and often had difficulty in breathing. She told me to lie down on the (7) _____ and gave me an (8) _____. First, she felt my (9) _____. Then she took my (10) _____, which was a bit high. Next she took my (11) _____. It was 37.9°C. Finally, she listened to my breathing through her (12) _____.

She didn't think there was anything seriously wrong with me – I was just a bit run down. So she wrote out a (13) _____ for some (14) _____ which she said would make me feel better. She also advised me, as she always did, to stop smoking and reminded me that if I didn't, then one day I might get (15) _____. As usual, I promised to try.

First aid

Artificial respiration (The kiss of life)

If an ill or injured person is not breathing, it is sometimes possible to start the breathing again by blowing air from your lungs into his or hers. As the body needs constant oxygen, you must begin artificial respiration (breathing) as soon as you discover that a casualty is not breathing.

Below is a step-to-step guide to how to give an adult artificial respiration. Unfortunately, the sentences are in the wrong order. Put them in the correct order by numbering them 1–10. The first one has been done for you.

☐ a blue-grey pallor towards pinkness. Give the first six to ten inflations fairly promptly, one after the other, then work according to the reaction of your casualty. If he is

☐ inflations coincide with his own breathing in, and continue until you feel that he can cope alone. It can seem hopeless

1 Lie the casualty on his* back and tilt back his head while supporting the back of his neck with the other hand. Keep

☐ recovery position[1] and watch to make sure that breathing continues.

☐ pinkish, he is probably getting enough oxygen so just keep going steadily. If he is still pale blue-grey, he is not getting an adequate supply of oxygen, so try to get more air into

☐ the chin up and blow air deeply and slowly into either the mouth or the nose (sealing the other to prevent air escaping) until the chest rises, showing that you have inflated

[1] The recovery position means lying face downwards with the head turned to one side and with the arm and leg on that side pulled up to prevent the casualty from flopping down completely on his front. The chin should also be pulled up to keep the airway clear.

* To avoid undue repetition of his or her, a male casualty has been assumed.

☐ to go on with artificial respiration but persistence is sometimes rewarded even after as long as an hour, so keep going (as long as the heart is beating).

When the casualty is breathing naturally, place him in the

☐ lungs. Watch the chest fall.

Repeat. If the heart is beating, the effect of the first few inflations should be a change in the casualty's colour from

☐ him quickly. But always wait for all the air to escape before you blow in again.

If the casualty begins to breathe again himself, let your

☐ the lungs. If the chest fails to rise, check that you have the casualty's head in the correct position. If it still does not rise after this, check for an obstruction in the airway.

Remove your mouth and allow the air to escape from the

Treatment in various situations and emergencies

Read through the list of situations and emergencies below, then decide how you would treat the casualties. Write the correct numbers (1–12) next to the words below.

an animal bite (not serious)	feeling faint
bruising	headaches, migraine
burns	a heart attack
choking	a nose-bleed
cramp	poisoning
drowning	a stroke

1 Reassure the casualty and let him or her rest in a half-sitting position with head and shoulders supported and knees bent. Put a cushion under them. To help get oxygen into the brain, loosen

any tight clothing around the throat, chest and waist. Send for an ambulance and while you wait, check the pulse rate every five or ten minutes and pass this information on to the ambulancemen.

2 If food has gone down the wrong way or a child has got something caught in his or her throat and coughing does not bring it up, slap him or her sharply on the back up to four times, between the shoulder blades.

3 All you can do is to try to minimize the effect of damage to the brain by keeping the patient breathing. Loosen clothing and support him or her in a half-sitting position with the head to one side, so that any saliva can drain away. Arrange for urgent removal to hospital. Do not give anything to eat or drink.

4 Do not waste time trying to clear water from the casualty's lungs but act at once. Do not even wait to get the casualty out of the water – only his or her head need be clear of it for you to begin artificial respiration – and after the first few inflations continue on dry land. If you are successful and breathing starts again, place the casualty in the recovery position and keep him or her warm. Take the casualty to hospital in case the lungs have been affected.

5 If it breaks the skin it should be well cleaned with cotton wool squeezed out in warm water or with a weak antiseptic solution.

6 Place a cold compress on the sufferer's forehead and get him or her to lie down, preferably somewhere quiet and dark. Also give him or her a mild painkiller, such as aspirin.

7 Sit the patient quietly, head bent forward to prevent blood running back down the throat. Get him or her to pinch the soft part of the nostrils together. After ten minutes the patient may release his or her grip gently.

8 Apply a cold compress, e.g. ice cubes in a plastic bag, or even a pack of frozen peas to slow down the flow of blood and reduce the swelling.

9 There is little you can do yourself but if any liquid remains around the mouth, wash it away with cold water. If what has been swallowed is something corrosive such as bleach or acid, give sips of milk or water to dilute it and cool the lips and mouth but do not induce vomiting as this may cause the throat and mouth to be burned again as the chemical comes up. Get the casualty to hospital.

10 Advise the person to sit down, put his or her head between his or her knees and take deep breaths.

11 Straighten out the affected part and then massage gently to ease the muscle.

12 The main thing to remember is to cool the injured part at once by running or pouring cold water over it. Even covering with wet towels or handkerchiefs will help. Continue this for at least fifteen minutes. If it still hurts after an hour, seek medical advice.

Follow up

What would you do if someone
- had fainted
- had hiccups
- had a hangover
- had swallowed a coin or a paper clip
- had frostbite

Useful verbs to do with health 1

Match up the verbs 1–16 with the most suitable endings a–p. Write your answers in the boxes at the bottom of the page.

1 amputate		a	against diseases
2 convalesce		b	your ankle
3 cure		c	a baby
4 cut		d	penicillin into the bloodstream
5 deaden		e	after an illness
6 deliver		f	a heart or a kidney
7 dislocate		g	someone back to health
8 dress		h	a leg
9 inject		i	a muscle
10 inoculate		j	your shoulder
11 nick		k	yourself with a knife
12 nurse		l	the disease
13 prescribe		m	a wound
14 pull		n	the pain
15 sprain/twist		o	yourself shaving
16 transplant		p	some medicine

1	2	3	4	5	6	7	8	9	10	11	12	13	14	15	16

Useful verbs to do with health 2

Fill in the missing verbs in the sentences below. Choose from the following and make any changes where necessary. Use each verb once only.

ache	disfigure	infect	suffer from
blister	disinfect	injure	suffocate
bruise	faint	lose consciousness	swell up
choke	fracture	maim	treat
contaminate	have a relapse	recuperate	vaccinate
diagnose	heal	sterilize	X-ray

1 She seemed to be getting better when suddenly she _____ and within a week was dead.

2 My mother is now _____ at a private nursing home after her operation.

3 A fairly common way of _____ rheumatism is to give the patient a cortisone injection.

4 The doctor _____ her illness as leukaemia.

5 I went running last night and I've been _____ ever since.

6 My sister has _____ hay fever since she was twelve.

7 They deliberately _____ the rats with the disease in order to test the effectiveness of the new drug.

8 She almost _____ to death on a chicken bone.

9 The leg could be broken. I think we'd better _____ it, just to make sure.

10 I remember vaguely seeing the doctor's face before I _____. The next thing I remember was waking up in a hospital bed.

11 The cut looks nasty. We'd better wash it and _____ it immediately.

12 When a mosquito bit her, her whole foot _____.

13 Two soldiers on parade _____ in the hot sun.

14 When he played his first game of tennis for a long time, his hand _____ because he wasn't used to holding the racket.

15 Two hundred people were killed and thousands _____ in the recent earthquake in Mexico.

16 She asked the doctor to _____ her children against measles.

17 He _____ his leg in two places when he fell down the stairs.

18 She _____ her knee when she banged her leg against the table.

19 She survived the plane crash but was _____ for life and will never walk again.

20 His wound has now _____ completely and it hasn't even left a scar.

21 Her face was badly _____ in the fire.

22 We were told not to eat the food because it had been _____ by rats.

23 The room was really hot and all the windows were closed. At one point I felt I was going to _____.

24 Before the operation all the materials and tools were carefully _____ to kill any bacteria.

Other useful words to do with health

Fill in the missing words in the sentences below. Choose from the following:

alternative medicine	feverish	operating theatre
antidote	germs	paralysis
blood transfusion	infectious	plastic surgery
check-up	injection	post-mortem
contagious	intensive-care unit	quarantine
dose	invalid	side-effects
epidemic		sufferer

1 If you have an _____ disease, such as a cold, others can catch it from you even if they don't touch you.

2 He's a surgeon and spends most of his time in the _____.

3 A _____ showed that he had died of food poisoning.

4 Summer is a nightmare for my wife as she's a hay fever _____.

5 Acupuncture, herbal medicine, osteopathy and homeopathy are examples of _____.

6 She had lost so much blood in the car crash that she had to be given a _____.

7 He's very seriously ill and has been moved to the hospital's _____.

8 If you bring a dog or a cat into Britain from abroad, it has to spend six months in _____, just to make sure it isn't suffering from any diseases.

9 My cousin is diabetic and has to have an insulin _____ every day.

10 She's been bitten by a snake. Unless she's given an _____ soon, she could die.

11 One of the _____ of this drug is that your hair falls out.

12 Thousands of old people died in the latest flu _____ to sweep through the country.

13 He went to the doctor for his annual _____.

14 Her face was so badly disfigured in the fire that she needed _____.

15 'I've been feeling very _____, doctor,' he explained, 'and I've also been having these pains in my chest.'

16 A _____ disease in one that can be passed on from person to person by touch.

17 She never fully recovered after the accident and spent the rest of her life as an _____.

18 According to the television advert, this disinfectant kills all known household _____.

19 Take one _____ of this cough mixture three times a day.

56

20 This disease can cause temporary _____ of the right arm and leg.

In other words...

(a) Match the statements 1–10 with suitable idioms a–j. Write your answers in the boxes at the bottom of the page.

1 The book was a best-seller and the author earned over £1 million.

2 The criminal told the police everything about the robbery.

3 Her mother is President of the company.

4 Janet always gets up very early.

5 'I'm a great actress. I'm probably one of the best of my generation!'

6 'I'm going to work harder. I really must.'

7 She's a very lively child.

8 'I hope he phones soon. I'm really worried and nervous.'

9 'I don't feel very well today.'

10 'My mother looks exactly like Margaret Thatcher.'

a She's an early bird.

b She's full of beans.

c She's a bit under the weather.

d She's decided to pull her socks up.

e She's a big shot.

f She's the spitting image of her.

g She's blowing her own trumpet.

h She made a bomb.

i She's on tenterhooks.

j She spilt the beans.

1	2	3	4	5	6	7	8	9	10

(b) Now complete the following six dialogues with a suitable idiom. Choose from the list on page 57 and make any necessary changes.

1 A: Do you want to pass this exam or not?

   B: Of course I do!

   A: Then you'd better _____, otherwise you're going to fail.

2 A: Have you heard if you've got the job yet?

   B: No, I'm still waiting and I'm really _____.

3 A: You're up early, Ken.

   B: Not really. I've always been a bit of _____.

4 A: You look a bit _____ today, Nick.

   B: Yes, I know. I think I'm going down with flu or something.

5 A: How come he's so wealthy?

   B: Well, apparently, he _____ in the 'eighties buying and selling flats in London's Docklands.

6 A: Have you noticed something about Mr North?

   B: No, what?

   A: Well, he's _____ of Prince Charles – especially the ears.

   B: Yes, you're right! He does look like him, doesn't he?

Section Three:
Crime and punishment

Crimes and offences 1

Match the crimes and offences 1–16 with the correct definitions a–p.
Write your answers in the boxes on the next page.

1 Arson

2 Assault

3 Blackmail

4 Burglary

5 Embezzlement

6 Forgery

7 Fraud

8 Hijacking

9 Kidnapping

10 Libel

11 Manslaughter

12 Murder

13 Rape

14 Robbery

15 Shoplifting

16 Theft

a is taking a person away by force and keeping them prisoner, usually in order to demand money for their safe return.

b is the serious crime of stealing large amounts of money from a bank, a shop or a vehicle, often using force or threats of violence.

c is the crime of copying things such as banknotes, letters, official documents, etc. in order to deceive people.

d is killing a person by accident or negligence.

e is forcing someone to have sex with you.

f is the crime of deliberately setting fire to a building.

g is taking control of an aeroplane, train, etc. by force, usually in order to make political demands.

h is killing a person deliberately.

i is demanding money or favours from someone by threatening to reveal a secret about them which, if made public, could cause the person embarrassment and harm.

j is deliberately taking goods from a shop without paying for them.

k is stealing money that is placed in your care, often over a period of time.

l is the crime of getting money from someone by tricking or deceiving them.

m is the crime of physically attacking someone.

n is printing or publishing something which is untrue and damages another person's reputation in some way.

o is the crime of breaking into a house, a flat, etc. in order to steal things.

p is the crime of stealing.

1	2	3	4	5	6	7	8	9	10	11	12	13	14	15	16

Crime and offences 2

Match the crimes and offences 1–16 with the correct definitions a–p. Write your answers in the boxes on page 62.

1 Assassination

2 Bribery and corruption

a is bad or improper behaviour by a person in a position of authority or trust, such as a doctor, dentist, police officer, etc.

3 Drug trafficking

4 Hit and run

5 Looting

6 Misconduct

7 Mugging

8 Perjury

9 Pickpocketing

10 Pilfering

11 Slander

12 Smuggling

13 Terrorism

14 Treason

15 Trespassing

16 Vandalism

b is stealing things from people's pockets or handbags, usually in crowds or in public places.

c is saying something untrue about someone with the intention of damaging his or her reputation.

d is deliberately damaging public buildings and other public property, usually just for the fun of it.

e is offering money or gifts to someone in a position of authority, e.g. a government official, in order to persuade them to help you in some way.

f is the crime of lying in court while giving evidence, when you have promised to tell the truth.

g is the crime of taking things or people illegally into or out of a country.

h is murdering a public figure such as a king, a president, etc.

i is entering privately owned land or property without the permission of the owner.

j is attacking someone, usually in a public place, in order to rob him or her.

k is trading in illegal drugs such as heroin, cannabis, cocaine, LSD, etc.

l is the crime of betraying your own country by helping its enemies.

m is stealing small amounts of goods or things of little value, often over a long period of time.

n is a car accident in which the guilty driver does not stop to help.

o is the use of violence such as murder and bombing in order to obtain political demands or to influence a government.

p is stealing from shops, buildings, etc. left unprotected after a violent event or a natural disaster such as an earthquake.

1	2	3	4	5	6	7	8	9	10	11	12	13	14	15	16

Follow up

Fill in the missing crimes and offences in the sentences below. Choose from the words in the previous two exercises.

1 The chief cashier admitted taking £30,000 of the firm's money during the previous three years and was found guilty of _____.

2 She sued the newspaper for _____ when it printed a story about her in which it claimed she had once been arrested for taking drugs.

3 The supermarket decided to install closed-circuit television in order to combat the problem of _____.

4 This is the sixth fire in the area in the past month. The police suspect _____.

5 He pleaded not guilty to murder but guilty to _____, saying that the gun had gone off and killed his wife by accident.

6 There have been so many cases of _____ in the street recently that the police are advising residents to install alarms and to notify neighbours when they go out.

7 The customs officer found nearly £20,000 worth of cut diamonds hidden in the man's guitar case. He was arrested and charged with _____.

8 Pop stars and famous people often employ bodyguards for themselves and members of their families as they are constantly worried about _____.

9 Most people of my generation remember the _____ of President Kennedy in Dallas in November 1963.

10 It looked like a real £20 note but on closer examination you could see that it was a very clever _____.

Criminals and wrongdoers

Match the criminals and wrongdoers 1–16 with the correct definitions a–p. Write your answers in the boxes on the next page.

1 An accomplice

2 An assassin

3 A burglar

4 A charlatan

5 A criminal

6 A forger

7 An imposter

8 A juvenile delinquent

9 A mugger

10 A poacher

11 A ringleader

a attacks people in the street and steals their money or other possessions.

b takes goods from shops without paying for them.

c deliberately damages public property, often because they are bored or enjoy doing it.

d murders someone important, such as a king or a president.

e leads others to do wrong or to make trouble.

f is someone who steals (usually without violence).

12 A robber

13 A shoplifter

14 A thief

15 A traitor

16 A vandal

g helps another person to commit a crime.

h deceives others by pretending to have special skills or knowledge, especially about medicine.

i steals from banks, shops, etc., usually planning them in advance in great detail.

j makes copies of money, letters, documents, etc. in order to deceive people.

k betrays his or her country.

l deceives people by pretending to be someone else.

m breaks into houses, shops, etc. in order to steal things.

n is a young person who has broken the law.

o catches or shoots animals, fish or birds on private land without permission.

p is someone who is guilty of a crime (or several crimes).

1	2	3	4	5	6	7	8	9	10	11	12	13	14	15	16

More criminals and people to do with crime and wrongdoing

Match up the people 1–16 with the correct definitions a–p. Write your answers in the boxes on the next page.

1 A drug addict/ a junkie

2 An assailant

3 A bigamist

4 A conspirator

5 A culprit

6 A hostage

7 An informer

8 A murderer

9 An offender

10 A pickpocket

11 A recidivist

12 A smuggler

13 A stowaway

14 A swindler

15 A victim

16 A witness

a is a formal or legal word for someone who is guilty of a crime.

b takes things or people illegally into or out of a country.

c deceives others in order to get money from them.

d gives information to the police in return for money.

e is unable to stop himself or herself from taking drugs.

f hides on board a ship or inside a plane in order to get a free ride.

g sees a crime being committed.

h is the person blamed for a crime or for doing something wrong.

i is a formal or legal word for someone who attacks another person.

j is someone who has been attacked or against whom a crime has been committed.

k is kept as a prisoner by a person or organization and may be killed if people don't do what the person or organization are demanding.

l steals things from people's pockets and handbags in crowded places.

m takes part in a secret plan to do something against the law.

n   keeps going back to a life of crime even after being punished. In other words, an incurable criminal.

o   marries illegally because he or she is already married to someone else.

p   deliberately kills someone.

1	2	3	4	5	6	7	8	9	10	11	12	13	14	15	16

Follow up

Read through the following newspaper extracts and fill in the missing words in the headlines. The word is either a type of crime or a type of criminal. Choose from the words in the previous five exercises.

1

_____ CAUGHT IN CELLAR

Last night the police broke into the cellar of a house in Highgate and found thousands of newly-made twenty pound notes which

2

_____ IN PEMBROKE PARK

The mutilated body of 19-year-old Sam Robertson was found yesterday in Pembroke Park. The police say he was stabbed fourteen times with

3

DARING _____ FROM NATIONAL GALLERY

A famous painting by the Dutch artist, Rembrandt, has disappeared from the National Gallery in London. It was taken some time during the night of August 3rd. The police think it may be the work of an international gang of

4

FIFTH _____ IN WILSON DRIVE

When Mr and Mrs Simmons returned home last night from the theatre they found that someone had broken into their house and taken a TV set, a video, £250 and a valuable diamond necklace. This is the fifth

66

5

_____ CAUGHT IN PHONE BOX

28-year-old Dwight Kelly was caught last night by detectives when he tried to pick up £250,000 from a phone box in Manchester. This was the sum he had demanded for the safe return of the 7-year-old son of property millionaire Frank Groves who

6

BANK _____ CAUGHT BY LOCAL DOG

When a man walked into Barclays Bank in Brighton and demanded £10,000 from the cashier he got the shock of his life when a huge Alsatian dog suddenly attacked him. It belonged to one of the bank's customers who was waiting in the queue. When he realised what was happening he immediately told his dog, Prince, to

7

91-YEAR-OLD _____ TOOK CLOTHES FOR GRAND-DAUGHTER'S BIRTHDAY PRESENT

91-year-old Agnes Drew took £40 worth of clothes from Marks & Spencer to give to her 16-year-old granddaugher, Carol, for her birthday.

'I couldn't afford to buy her anything,' she said, 'so I decided to

8

_____ FREED

Teresa Black, the 17-year-old schoolgirl and her boyfriend, 21-year-old David Barker who were captured by guerillas while on holiday in Nepal, have been allowed to go free. A spokesman for the

9

_____ ATTEMPT FOILED

Prince Charles came close to being shot yesterday afternoon while inspecting a factory in Gateshead. Police spotted a man with a high power rifle in the top window of a building minutes before the Prince was due to pass by. If he had not been spotted the chances are that

10

ACTRESS SUES FOR _____

Oscar-winning actress Amanda Milligan is suing the Daily Mirror newspaper for _____ after an article was published last Saturday claiming that Miss Milligan had undergone extensive plastic surgery to alter her looks and figure. This is not the first time

Idioms to do with crime

(a) *Match the idioms 1–15 with the correct definitions a–o. Write your answers in the boxes on the page opposite.*

1 a con trick

2 a fence

3 an inside job

4 blow the whistle on someone/something

5 case a joint

6 catch someone red-handed

7 cook the books

8 do a bunk

9 do time

10 fall off the back of a lorry

11 go straight

12 get off scot-free

13 grease someone's palm

14 joy-riding

15 launder money

a (of goods) to be stolen

b bribe someone

c discover someone in the act of committing a crime

d a dishonest trick played on someone in order to get money from them

e legitimize money obtained illegally

f publicly reveal something illegal or dishonest

g stealing a car and driving it, often dangerously, just for fun

h examine or inspect the place you intend to rob

i someone who buys and sells stolen goods

j avoid punishment completely

k falsify a company's accounts; cheat at bookkeeping

l a crime committed by someone connected with the place or organisation where the crime took place

m serve a prison sentence

n give up a criminal way of life; not break the law again

o disappear without telling anyone where you are going

1	2	3	4	5	6	7	8	9	10	11	12	13	14	15

(b) Complete the following sentences with a suitable idiom. Choose from the ones listed above and make changes to the verbs where necessary.

1 The police _____ the thieves _____ as they were leaving the shop through a back window.

2 The mysterious disappearance of one of the cashiers shortly after the robbery confirmed the police's suspicions that it had been an _____ .

3 He only got the contract because he _____ a government official's _____ .

4 He had been _____ for years, trying to cover up the £10,000 he had taken from the company.

5 When Tom came out of prison after serving two years, he promised his girlfriend that he would _____ and never steal again.

6 A few years ago, my cousin _____ for fraud. He was in prison for three years altogether.

7 Don't buy those cassette recorders. If they're that cheap they must have _____ .

8 Although the police knew they had committed the crime, they couldn't prove it, so the men _____ .

9 Most bank robbers _____ thoroughly before attempting to rob it.

10 He _____ in the middle of the night to avoid paying his hotel bill.

Law and order: The police

Look at the drawings below and write the correct numbers 1–13 next to the following words.

bullet-proof vest	notebook	uniform
fingerprint	police officers	visor
handcuffs	riot shield	walkie talkie
helmet	torch	
magnifying glass	truncheon	

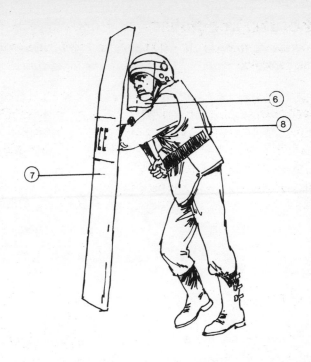

Law and order: In court

Fill in the missing words in the passage below. Choose from the following and note that two of the words are used twice.

accused	guilty	put on probation
acquitted	imprisonment	sentence
barristers	judge	testimony
Crown Court	jury	trial
defence	Justice of the Peace	verdict
dock	Magistrates Court	witness box
evidence	oath	witnesses
fine	prosecution	

There are two main courts of law in Britain – the (1) _____ for minor offences, such as speeding, shoplifting, etc. and the (2) _____ for more serious offences such as fraud and murder. The magistrate or (3) _____ who tries cases in the lower court does not have special education or training in law and does not get a salary. (The job is voluntary and part-time.)

At a (4) _____ at a Crown Court, the (5) _____ or defendant stands in the (6) _____ while lawyers question (7) _____ who have to say what they have seen or know and who stand in the (8) _____. They have to swear an (9) _____ to 'tell the truth, the whole truth and nothing but the truth.' What they say is known as their (10) _____.

There are usually two lawyers or (11) _____ in the courtroom. One is known as Counsel for the (12) _____, who speaks for the defendant, and the other as Counsel for the (13) _____. This person has to try to prove that the person accused of the crime really committed it.

The (14) _____ sits in a large seat facing the defendant and wears a special gown and wig. He or she does not decide whether an accused person is guilty or not. This is left to the (15) _____, made up of twelve members of the public, to decide. During the trial they sit in silence, listening carefully to all the (16) _____ . Then, they are locked away until they can decide whether the person is (17) _____ or not (18) _____ . This decision is called the (19) _____ .

The (20) _____ now decides the punishment or (21) _____ as it is called. If the person is innocent, he or she is (22) _____ , which means that he or she is released immediately and is free to go home. If the person is guilty and the crime is serious, he or she could be given several years (23) _____ . However, if it is a first offence, the person might be given a (24) _____ instead, for example £1,000, or (25) _____ .

The verdict is yours

Work in pairs or groups of three. You are going to be judges. Read through the list of crimes below and then decide the type of sentence you think the person ought to get. Before starting, here is a list of possible sentences. You can choose from these or decide on your own.

The death penalty
   You could sentence the person to death (by hanging, the death chamber, electric chair, guillotine, etc.) Note: the death penalty has been abolished in the U.K.
Life imprisonment
   You could imprison the person for life.
Imprisonment
   You could imprison the person for a set period (decide how many months or years).
Fines
   You could fine the person (decide the amount).
Put on probation
   You could put the person on probation, e.g. for 3 years. (This means you don't go to prison. Instead you have to keep out of trouble and report to a probation officer every week during the period of the sentence.)

Suspended sentence

You could give the person a suspended sentence, e.g. 2 years suspended sentence. (This means the person is given a two year prison sentence but only has to serve it if he or she commits another crime during that period.)

Acquit/let off

You could let the person off with a caution.

Do community service

You could give the person community service. (He or she has to do socially useful work, e.g. helping handicapped children or old people instead of going to prison).

Driving ban/endorsement

If a driving offence, you could ban the person from driving (decide how long) or endorse his or her licence, which means that you mark in it that the person has broken the law.

1 A person who robbed a shop and wounded the owner with a knife.

2 A person who set fire to his or her flat for the insurance money.

3 A person in the Government who has been spying for a foreign power.

4 A person who took a bar of chocolate from a shop without paying for it.

5 A person who bought a camera with a false cheque.

6 A person who murdered a policeman in cold blood.

7 A person who kidnapped a small child and held him to ransom. (The child was unhurt.)

8 A person who hi-jacked a plane. In the rescue attempt one passenger died of a heart attack.

9 A person caught selling cocaine and heroin.

10 A person who saw a woman being attacked, went to her aid and accidentally killed her attacker.

11 A person who refuses to do military service.

12 A person who stole a car, then crashed into another one, seriously injuring the driver.

13 A football supporter who threw a brick at a referee during a football match. (The brick struck the referee on the leg.)

14 A person who drove through a traffic light when it was showing red.

15 A person who got married when he already had a wife.

When you have finished, compare your verdicts with other pairs or groups.

To talk about

What would happen in your country if you:
- were caught speeding?
- accidentally killed someone?
- were caught smoking marijuana?
- attacked and injured someone?
- were caught writing graffiti on a public building?
- were caught shoplifting?
- murdered someone?

Verbs to do with crime 1

Match the verbs on the left 1–16 with a suitable phrase a–p. Write your answers in the boxes on the next page.

1 accuse someone	a	in cold blood
2 arrest someone	b	into custody
3 ban	c	a witness
4 break	d	telephone boxes
5 charge someone	e	for armed robbery
6 commit	f	a prison sentence
7 cross-examine	g	a case

8 hijack	h with murder
9 hold up	i smoking in public places
10 murder someone	j of shoplifting
11 pinch	k the alarm
12 serve	l a crime
13 sound	m some money
14 take someone	n a plane
15 try	o the law
16 vandalize	p a bank

1	2	3	4	5	6	7	8	9	10	11	12	13	14	15	16

Verbs to do with crime 2

Fill in the missing verbs in the sentences below. Choose from the following and make any changes where necessary. Use each verb once only.

acquit	deport	mug	shoplift
assault	double-cross	pilfer	smuggle
blackmail	embezzle	prosecute	sue
burgle	imprison	prove	swindle
convict	interrogate	reprieve	threaten
defraud	kidnap	rob	trespass

1 An armed gang _____ the Kingsway Road branch of Barclays bank yesterday afternoon and got away with nearly £90,000.

2 The salesman was very persuasive and managed to _____ the elderly couple out of their life savings.

3 Tourists have been advised to avoid going off into the mountains as six people have been _____ in the past month. As yet, no-one has been freed.

4 The man was _____ from Britain to Germany where he will face charges of terrorism and murder.

5 The youths were fined £300 for _____ on Government property and deliberately causing damage to expensive machinery.

6 She had pleaded not guilty throughout the trial, so it was a relief when the jury finally _____ her.

7 The judge _____ him for ten years for fraud.

8 The prisoner was _____ just hours before he was due to be executed.

9 The robbers _____ to shoot anyone who tried to sound the alarm.

10 The politician was being _____ by a man who claimed he had photographs of him accepting bribes.

11 Blake _____ the others in the gang and escaped to South America with most of the money from the robbery.

12 The cleaner was caught _____ towels and glasses from the hotel.

13 He threatened to _____ her for every penny she had if she tried to break her contract.

14 It would be easy to _____ my father's house as he always leaves his bedroom window open during the day.

15 As the man left the shop, the store detective stopped him and accused him of _____. He had been caught on camera stuffing three ties into his briefcase.

16 He was so disappointed that his team were losing that he ran onto the pitch and _____ the opposing team's goalkeeper, hitting him several times in the face.

17 He made large sums of money _____ refugees into Britain, Holland and Germany.

18 The post office clerk _____ nearly £5,000 over a period of two years.

19 She was walking through the park in broad daylight when a man _____ her, stealing her handbag containing nearly £200.

20 Although the police knew he was guilty, they were unable to _____ it – they just didn't have sufficient evidence.

21 She was _____ of manslaughter and sent to prison for five years.

22 The detectives _____ the suspect for nearly ten hours before finally letting him go.

23 The two directors _____ the company of nearly £2 million.

24 There was a large sign on the outside of the building which said: 'Trespassers will be _____'.

Other useful words to do with crime

Fill in the missing words in the sentences below. Choose from the following:

abolished	coroner	inquest	loot
alibi	custody	internment	martial law
amnesty	damages	judicial	on parole
bail	euthanasia	justice	statement
clues	illicit	law-abiding	warder
conviction	injunction	legislation	warrant

1 The _____ of political prisoners is quite common in some countries. Britain tried it unsuccessfully in Northern Ireland to combat the IRA.

2 The government is thinking of introducing _____ making it compulsory for every citizen to carry an identity card.

3 A person who looks after prisoners is called a prison officer or a _____.

4 Since there was something very suspicious about the man's sudden death, the _____ was called in and an _____ was held at the Town Hall.

5 In Britain, capital punishment in the form of death by hanging was _____ in 1969.

6 The court issued an _____ forbidding the newspaper from publishing any more photographs of the Princess of Wales at a private Health Club.

7 The police have issued a _____ for her arrest.

8 Trial by jury is an important part of the British system of _____.

9 The new governor issued a general _____ to all the rebels.

10 After the unsuccessful attempt to overthrow the government, the whole country was put under _____ for a month.

11 His _____ for the night of the murder was that he had been at his girlfriend's, watching TV.

12 He successfully sued the newspaper for libel and was awarded nearly £50,000 in _____.

13 The judge refused to grant him _____, as it was feared that he would try to leave the country before his trial came up.

14 Before the police took him away, the thief told his wife where he had hidden the _____.

15 They were prosecuted for dealing in _____ substances.

16 The doctor was found guilty of _____ when he turned off the life-support system of a patient who was terminally ill with cancer.

17 The police took down the man's _____, read it back to him, then asked him to sign it.

18 Detectives still haven't found any _____ as to the whereabouts of the two missing 13-year-old schoolchildren.

19 The robbers were taken to the police station and held in _____ until their trial.

20 She couldn't possibly have done it. She's the most honest, _____ citizen I've ever met.

21 This was his seventh _____ for stealing cars.

22 Not all countries have the same political or _____ systems.

23 He was released _____ to go to his mother's funeral.

Sort out the texts

There are two unusual crime stories below. Unfortunately they are all mixed up. Try to sort them out by putting the sections in the correct order. Number the first story 1–7 and the second one 8–13. (Number 1 has already been identified for you.)

○ worked out that the best way of entry was through the roof. There was, however, the slight problem

○ gang were forced to flee before they even had a chance to enter the building.

○ **THE QUICKEST BANK ROBBERY DETECTION**
When Eddie Blake slid a note to the

○ that it lay directly beneath an over-head railway line near London Bridge Station.
Undeterred, the gang dug out

○ demand note had been written on the back of an envelope with his name and address on it.

80

○ a bag and hand it over.'
The girl did as she was asked and within minutes Blake was

○ the amount needed, and the resulting explosion closed three mainline stations for four hours, stranded

(1) **THE MOST CONSPICUOUS BREAK-IN ATTEMPT**
A gang, determined to rob a Bermondsey tobacco warehouse,

○

○ when he arrived breathlessly home, the police were waiting for him. His

○ thousands of commuters and brought rush-hour traffic to a complete standstill. The noise attracted police from a wide area, and the

○

○ running through the crowded streets with his haul. An hour later,

○ the gravel between the railway sleepers and filled it full of gelignite. They slightly overestimated

○ cashier of a Nevada bank the message was clear. 'This is a hold-up.' it announced. 'Put all the money into

In other words...

(a) Match up the statements 1–10 with a suitable idiom a–j. Write your answers in the boxes on the next page.

1 I don't really like opera.

2 I hate the rude way in which he talks to his mother. It really angers me.

3 Amanda Redman? The name sounds familiar.

a It's spick and span.

b It's all Greek to me.

c It's not my cup of tea.

d It's bucketing down.

e It gets my goat.

f It's going for a song.

4 We were almost killed.

5 Her flat is very clean and tidy.

6 It won't take me long to do it. It's very easy.

7 That building is very ugly to look at.

8 It's raining heavily.

9 I don't understand a word of it!

10 That car's very cheap to buy.

g It rings a bell.

h It's a piece of cake.

i It was a close shave.

j It's an eyesore.

1	2	3	4	5	6	7	8	9	10

(b) Now complete the following six dialogues with a suitable idiom. Choose from the above list and make any necessary changes.

1 A: Do you know Pauline Brown?

   B: Well, the name certainly _____. Isn't she something to do with politics?

2 A: What's the weather like, Pam?

   B: It's _____ at the moment.

   A: Typical! There goes our picnic, then!

3 A: Do you like football?

   B: No, it's not really _____. I prefer golf.

4 A: What was he talking about?

   B: I've no idea. It was _____.

5 A: Was the exam difficult?

   B: No, it was _____.

6 A: You look annoyed, Mandy.

   B: I am. It's Nick. I don't mind giving him a lift to work but what _____ is the fact that he's never once offered to pay for the petrol.

Check 1

This is a check to see how many words you can remember from Section One, Section Two and Section Three. Try to do it without looking back at the previous pages.

1 He deliberately lives alone, away from other people. He's
_____ .

(a) a hermit (b) an atheist (c) a miser (d) a sceptic

2 Which of the following people is not young?

(a) an adolescent (b) a veteran (c) an infant (d) a juvenile

3 She spent three years as _____ on a desert island before
a passing ship rescued her.

(a) an expatriate (b) a scapegoat (c) a squatter

(d) a castaway

4 Which person is on strike?

(a) a deserter (b) a conscientious objector (c) a picket

(d) a blackleg

5 She's such _____ . It's hard to get a word in edgeways
when she's around.

(a) a tomboy (b) a chatterbox (c) a big shot (d) a busybody

6 He believes everything you tell him. He's really _____ .

(a) gullible (b) absent-minded (c) shrewd (d) highly-strung

7 She thinks a lot of herself and her abilities. She's very
_____ .

(a) aggressive (b) pompous (c) talented (d) conceited

8 I never walk under a ladder because it's unlucky. I'm very
_____ about things like that.

(a) narrow-minded (b) weak-willed (c) superstitious

(d) obstinate

9 He felt very _____ when he first went to live abroad. He missed everything, especially his family and friends.

(a) homesick   (b) nostalgic   (c) disillusioned   (d) heartbroken

10 Which person is very angry?

(a) She's annoyed.   (b) She's furious.   (c) She's bad-tempered.
(d) She's touchy.

11 In each of the following groups of four words, one does not fit in. <u>Underline</u> the word and try to say why it is different from the rest.

(a) hospitable, considerate, well-mannered, spiteful

(b) scared, baffled, apprehensive, petrified

(c) nostril, temple, thigh, lobe

(d) bandage, ointment, truncheon, sling

(e) busker, midwife, chiropodist, surgeon

(f) flu, measles, malaria, asthma

(g) kidney, knuckle, intestines, windpipe

12 There are twelve words hidden in the following square. They are all jobs. See how many you can find. You can read vertically (5 words), horizontally (5 words) or diagonally (2 words).

```
A B E D F R O G M A N I J U N F
K R T A N B F O P H E G Q J T O
C O M J W L I B R I B S D U R M
S K I L P A M U G G L N E D E B
D E T E C T I V E O S K R G W O
E R I D R U C O N C A N S E D S
N I C C R I T I C G B R U S H F
A L B E R P A H M O N I C F R G
N F G R C E D U D W M N U R S E
N O L T A J I C Q U I P V I N M
Y D E S E R H A M S M H O T K S
R O T D A D V U C P A T T S D E
T B I L I V I P E S T E S O E G
A F W E S T C A R J R O V I N R
G I L B D O O I H M O L A D I N
F A U D I T O R E N N P I C A F
```

13 Read through the following sentences and try to work out what the missing words are. To help you, the first and last letters of the words are given.

  (a) She stuffs dead animals. She's a t_____t.

  (b) He's suffering from i_____a and finds it very difficult to get to sleep at night.

  (c) He was so badly injured in the car accident that they had to a_____e his leg.

  (d) This drug has no known s_____e e_____s, so it's perfectly safe to use.

  (e) She went to the o_____n's to have her eyes tested.

  (f) She almost c_____d on a fishbone.

  (g) I'm p_____t. The baby's due in December.

  (h) Give her a t_____r – that should help calm her down.

  (i) Another word for 'word-blindness' is d_____a.

  (j) If you don't like the shape of your nose you can have it changed through p_____c s_____y.

  (k) The doctor wrote out a p_____n for some medicine.

14 Match the words on the left with the words on the right. Draw lines between the correct pairs.

assassination	death by accident
arson	tell lies in court
blackmail	a false cheque
burglary	set fire to buildings
fraud	betray one's country
kidnapping	break into a house
manslaughter	political murder
libel	demand a ransom
perjury	threaten to reveal a secret
treason	printing lies

15 Say whether the following sentences are correct (C) or incorrect (I).

  (a) The captain of the ship found a **stowaway** hiding in one of the lifeboats.

  (b) He must be a **gatecrasher**. He certainly wasn't invited to the party.

  (c) He reads a lot. He's very **illiterate**.

  (d) She had lots of **crow's feet** on her stomach.

  (e) He punched the man three times in the face. Now he's facing a charge of **assault**.

  (f) **Bashful** people are usually full of self-confidence.

  (g) Another word for magistrate is **Justice of the Peace** or **JP** for short.

  (h) **I got it for a song**. It was really expensive.

  (i) He helped me rob the bank. He was my **accomplice**.

  (j) These shirts are stolen. **They fell off the back of a lorry**.

  (k) He's in charge of the exam. He's the **adjudicator**.

  (l) He makes sure people at the swimming baths don't drown. He's a **bodyguard**.

16 Complete the following sentences using a suitable part of the body used as a verb.

  (a) She _____ her way through to the front of the queue.

  (b) The Prime Minister urged the back benchers to _____ the line and vote with the government.

  (c) He tried to _____ me off with an out-of-date machine.

  (d) Could you _____ me the screwdriver, please?

  (e) They left me to _____ the bill.

  (f) I could never be a surgeon. I can't _____ blood.

17 Look at the drawings below and write down what is wrong with
   each person.

(a) He's _____ .   (b) She's _____ .

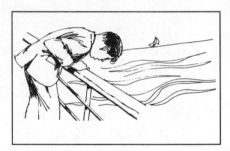

(c) She's _____ .   (d) He's _____ .

(e) She's _____ .

18 Match up the verbs on the right with the words on the left. Draw lines between the correct pairs.

(a)

cure	a shoulder
deliver	a muscle
dislocate	a disease
dress	medicine
pull	a wound
prescribe	a baby

(b)

accuse someone	from driving
arrest someone	into custody
ban someone	of theft
charge someone	in cold blood
take someone	for arson
murder someone	with armed robbery

19 Name the following.

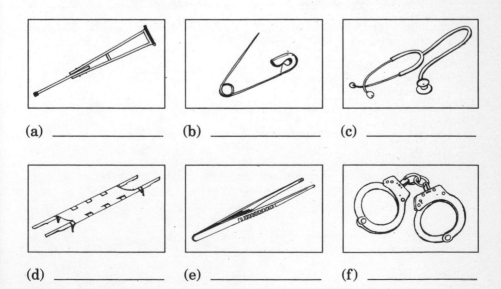

(a) _____

(b) _____

(c) _____

(d) _____

(e) _____

(f) _____

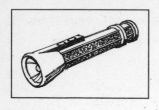 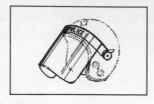 

(g) _____ (h) _____ (i) _____

(j) _____

20 Rewrite the following sentences with suitable idioms. (The idiom should include the word in brackets after each sentence.)

(a) Seeing young people deliberately damaging phone boxes really *makes me angry*. (blood)

(b) I was *really frightened*. (leaf)

(c) I found it difficult *not to laugh* when he tried to sing. He was so out of tune! (face)

(d) I'm *not feeling very well* today. (weather)

(e) Did you realise that your father *looks exactly like* Andrew Lloyd-Webber? (image)

(f) You've got to *make a greater effort* if you want to pass the exam. (socks)

(g) He *earned a lot of money* with his first novel. (bomb)

(h) We *bribed the official* to get the contract. (palm)

(i) The examination was *really easy*. (cake)

(j) That was a *narrow escape*! We could have been killed. (shave)

21 Here are thirty words in alphabetical order. Write each word under the correct heading (five words under each).

amnesia	enthusiastic	robbery
callous	genius	ruthless
charlatan	hijacking	sadist
cheeky	imposter	sensible
concussion	indigestion	slander
cramp	loyal	sponger
crank	malicious	traitor
creative	nausea	two-faced
culprit	patriot	understanding
embezzlement	perjury	vandal

Types of people

_____
_____
_____
_____
_____

Adjectives to describe people (negative)

_____
_____
_____
_____
_____

Adjectives to describe people (positive)

_____
_____
_____
_____
_____

Criminals and wrongdoers

_____
_____
_____
_____
_____

Diseases, illnesses and conditions

_____
_____
_____
_____
_____

Crimes and offences

_____
_____
_____
_____
_____

22 Unscramble the following words and match them with the definitions a–l below.

ant tewlkeb	gastociuon	piesnt	stevalire
dazmea	laviciin	quisten	sylacaut
festucfoa	misnadval	rimferno	tirannumtoil

(a) The upper part of the foot between the toes and the ankle.

(b) Having lots of different skills and abilities and being able to easily change from one kind of activity to another.

(c) Anyone who is not a soldier or any other member of the armed forces.

(d) Poor health caused by not eating enough food or by not eating enough of the right kinds of food.

(e) Someone who spoils the atmosphere or prevents others from enjoying themselves by being very boring and negative about everything.

(f) Someone who gives information to the police about crimes or criminals in return for money.

(g) Die because of lack of air.

(h) Someone who has been injured or killed in an accident, a fire or a war.

(i) So surprised that you find it hard to believe what has happened.

(j) An official inquiry to find out the cause of an unexpected or sudden death, especially when a crime is suspected.

(k) (*Of a disease*) That can be passed on from one person to another by touch.

(l) Deliberately damaging public buildings and other public property, usually just for the fun of it.

23 Complete the crossword with the missing verbs from the sentences below.

Across →

3 Two men _____ a British Airways plane and demanded to be flown to Libya.

5 She slipped while skating and _____ her ankle.

8 We can't drink the water in our well. Chemicals from a nearby factory have _____ it.

10 After smashing her father's car, she was too frightened to go home and _____ the music.

11 At present he is _____ a six year prison sentence for armed robbery.

12 The prosecution have to _____ that the accused is guilty.

13 I wasn't being serious, Jane. I was only _____ your leg.

16 My head _____. Have you got any aspirins?

17 The best way to _____ this illness is with penicillin.

18 It was the first time she had _____ the law.

20 The gang planned to _____ the bank at the weekend.

21 They planned to _____ the English football team and demand a ransom of £1 million for their safe return.

22 Fifty English football hooligans were _____ from Holland last night after causing considerable damage to the hotel they were staying at.

Down ↓

1 She _____ her skull when she fell down the stairs.

2 You should always _____ instruments before an operation.

4 His aunt went into a private nursing home to _____ after her illness.

5 'If you print that in your newspaper then I'll _____ you for libel!' the actress shouted at the journalist.

6 The doctor _____ his illness as mumps.

7 Have you been _____ against influenza this year?

8 More and more young people under thirteen are _____ crimes.

9 He was arrested for _____ a policeman. He had hit him in the face several times.

14 The judge _____ her for ten months.

15 The cut has finally _____ now. See, there's not even a scar.

19 Our house was _____ last week. Among the things stolen were a TV, a video and £200 in cash.

Section Four: Phrasal verbs

Phrasal verbs with 'down'

(a) *Complete the definitions below with a suitable phrasal verb. Choose from the following and make any changes where necessary.*

bring down	go down	pour down	settle down
close down	hold down	pull down	stand down
cut down	let down	put down	take down
get down	play down	run down	turn down

1 If it is _pour down_, it is raining very heavily.

2 If you _stand down_ from a job or position you resign or withdraw from it, usually to let someone else take your place.

3 When a ship _____, it sinks.

4 If you _____ a request, an offer, an invitation, etc, you refuse or say no to it.

5 If people or some event _____ a government, this means they are defeated and lose their power.

6 If you _____ someone _____, you disappoint that person by failing to do what he or she has been relying on you to do.

7 If you _____ someone you criticize or speak badly of him or her.

8 If you _____, for example, the number of cigarettes you smoke, you smoke less.

9 To _____ something is to write down or make notes on what someone is saying.

10 If you _____ a job, you manage to keep it, even though it might be difficult to do so.

11 If you _____ a building, you demolish or destroy it.

12 If a factory _____, it shuts permanently.

13 If you _____ something _____, you try to make it appear less important or serious than it really is.

14 If something _____ you _____, it makes you feel depressed.

15 If you _____, this usually means that you get married, set up home and start leading a quiet, routine life.

16 If a government _____ a revolt or rebellion, they crush it by force.

(b) *Now complete the following sentences with a suitable phrasal verb with 'down'. Choose from the verbs in exercise (a) and make any changes where necessary.*

1 The nuclear industry is always anxious to _____ the dangers of an accident at a nuclear power station.

2 There was a revolt in the north of the country, but government troops soon _____ it _____.

3 Ms Stevens was at a meeting, so her secretary _____ my message.

4 The cold weather and the rain is really _____ me _____. I wish it was summer!

5 There must be something wrong with Frank. He can't seem to _____ a job. This must be the third time he's been sacked in the past year.

6 I'll probably _____ when I'm about thirty-five. I'm not old enough to get married and start a family yet.

7 If this news leaks out it could be damaging enough to _____ the government – if not now, certainly at the next election.

8 You'd better take an umbrella with you, it's _____ outside.

9 She was offered an excellent job in Canada, but _____ it _____ because she didn't want to leave Britain.

10 If the factory _____, more than 2,000 people will be out of work.

11 The *Titanic* _____ on her maiden voyage from Southampton to New York in 1912.

12 I think Mr Blake should _____ as chairman and let someone younger take over.

13 They've _____ those old buildings in Green Street to make way for a new supermarket.

14 'If you can't stop smoking completely, Mr James,' the doctor said as he examined his chest, 'then at least try and _____. Otherwise you'll probably get lung cancer one day.'

15 Now we're all relying on you, Nick, so please don't _____ us _____.

16 She's always _____ people _____. I don't think I've ever heard her say something nice about someone.

Phrasal verbs with 'in' and 'into'

(a) *Complete the definitions below with a suitable phrasal verb. Choose from the following and make any changes where necessary.*

break in	come into	look into	take in
bring in	fill in	put in	talk into
check in	hand in	run into	turn in
come in	join in	sink in	turn into

1 If you _____ something, such as an essay or an exercise, you give it to someone to read or correct.

2 If you _____ someone, you meet him or her unexpectedly.

3 To _____ means to go to bed.

4 When you _____ at a hotel, you register your name, address, etc, and pick up the key to your room.

5 To _____ means to enter a building by force or illegally, usually in order to steal.

6 If you _____ someone _____ doing something, you persuade him or her to do it.

7 If you _____ something, you investigate it.

8 To _____ money or property means to inherit it.

9 If someone or something _____ another thing, they change and become someone or something different.

10 If you _____ something, such as a game, you take part in it.

11 When a government _____ a new law, they introduce it.

12 If you _____ something, for example central heating, you install it.

13 If you _____ an item of clothing, you make it smaller and tighter.

14 If you _____ for someone, you do the work or take the place of that person during their absence.

15 When something _____, it becomes fashionable.

16 When something _____, for example an unpleasant piece of news, it gradually becomes understood.

(b) *Now complete the following sentences with a suitable phrasal verb with 'in' or 'into'. Choose from the verbs in exercise (a) and make any changes where necessary.*

1 The singer told the audience to _____ the chorus.

2 The news of her death was such a shock. It still hasn't really _____ yet.

3 In the fairy tale, when the princess kissed the frog it _____ a handsome prince.

4 Mr Kent's away this week, so they've asked me to _____ for him.

5 After we had _____, we went up to our room, unpacked our suitcases then went down to the hotel restaurant for a meal.

6 Guess who I _____ this week? Charles North! You remember, he was in our class at school. I haven't seen him for over ten years.

7 I didn't really want to go to the cinema, but they somehow managed to _____ me _____ it. I'm glad they did now as it was the best film I've seen for ages.

8 Thieves _____ over the weekend and stole three valuable paintings.

9 I'm feeling very tired. I think I'll _____.

10 The manager asked her assistant to _____ the complaint.

11 I'm old enough to remember when miniskirts first _____.

12 Since she had lost weight she had to _____ her clothes as they no longer fitted her.

13 He'll _____ a lot of money when his father dies.

14 The government are planning to _____ a law to raise the school leaving age to seventeen.

15 Last winter was so cold that they decided to _____ central heating and double glazing.

16 Before they left the examination room, the students _____ their answer sheets.

Phrasal verbs with 'off'

(a) *Complete the definitions below with a suitable phrasal verb.*
Choose from the following and make any changes where
necessary.

break off	kick off	see off	tell off
drop off	lay off	show off	turn off
go off	pull off	stop off	wear off
keep off	put off	take off	write off

1 When football players _____, they start the game.
2 If you _____ someone _____, you go with them to the airport, railway station, etc. and say goodbye to them there.
3 If you _____ someone _____, you scold or reprimand them for something they have done wrong.
4 If a bank _____ a loan, it regards the debt as a loss which will never be recovered.
5 If you _____ a relationship, you end it.
6 If you _____ something _____, you complete or perform something successfully.
7 If you _____ someone, you imitate or copy their speech, appearance or behaviour, usually to make others laugh.
8 If you _____ a machine or appliance, you stop it working by moving a switch or a button.
9 If a bomb _____, it explodes.
10 If a feeling _____, it becomes less intense or is no longer felt.
11 If you _____ someone _____, you distract them in some way or discourage them from doing something.
12 If you _____ a particular subject, you avoid talking about it.
13 If you _____ somewhere, you interrupt your journey to visit a friend, a shop, etc. for a short time.
14 If an employer _____ workers, they lose their jobs, often temporarily, because there is no more work for them to do.

15 To _____ means to fall asleep.
16 People who _____ try to impress others with their skills or abilities.

(b) *Now complete the following sentences with a suitable phrasal verb with 'off'. Choose from the verbs in exercise (a) and make any changes where necessary.*

1 His parents tried to _____ him _____ being an actor by saying how difficult it was and that only a small percentage ever found work or could make a living from it.
2 I _____ at the chemist's on my way home to pick up a prescription for my wife.
3 Don't forget to _____ all the downstairs lights before you go to bed.
4 Try to _____ the subject of war tonight if you can. You know it only upsets your Aunty Jean.
5 Because of the recession, the company had to _____ nearly three hundred workers.
6 We couldn't stop laughing when Sue suddenly stood up and started _____ the new boss. She was just like her.
7 Those countries are never going to be able to pay back their loans, so the banks will just have to _____ them _____.
8 We were all very surprised when Colin _____ his engagement, especially as he and Emily planned to marry in the summer.
9 She was so happy when she managed to _____ the biggest business deal in her life.
10 The manager _____ her _____ for arriving late again.
11 The headmaster's speech was so boring that I _____ half-way through it.
12 I hate the way he _____ on the football field. I don't know who he's trying to impress.

13 The effect of this drug should _____ in a couple of hours.

14 We _____ our friends _____ at the airport.

15 A loud cheer went up from the huge crowd as England _____ in their World Cup match against Germany.

16 We were just leaving the shop when the bomb _____. Fortunately, we weren't seriously hurt.

Complete the captions 1

Complete the captions in the drawings below using a suitable phrasal verb from the previous three exercises, namely ones with 'down', 'in', 'into' and 'off'.

1 He's _____ .

2 It's _____ .

3 She's _____ .

4 The water's been_____

_____ .

5 She's _____
  some money.

6 He's _____
  a message.

7 They're_____
  her_____ .

8 They've_____ .

9 They've just _____

_____ .

10 He's really _____

_____ .

11 She never_____ .

12 It's _____ .

13 She's _____
_____.

14 He's _____
a frog.

15 They're _____ it
_____.

Phrasal verbs with 'on'

(a) *Complete the definitions below with a suitable phrasal verb. Choose from the following and make any changes where necessary.*

bring on	count on	hold on	send on
call on	drag on	live on	take on
catch on	get on	look on	try on
come on	go on	pick on	turn on

1 If you _____ someone, you rely on them for their help and support.

2 If you _____ doing something, you continue doing it.

3 If you _____ while something happens, you watch it without taking part yourself.

4 If someone _____ you _____, they employ you.

5 If something _____, it takes much longer than seems necessary, which has the effect of making people bored, impatient or unhappy.

6 If something _____ an illness or physical discomfort, it is the cause of it.

7 If you ask someone to _____, you want them to wait for a short while.

8 When you _____ something, for example a television, you start it working.

9 If something _____, it becomes popular or fashionable.

10 If you _____ someone, you repeatedly and unfairly treat them badly, often by punishing them or giving them boring or unpleasant jobs to do.

11 If you _____ a piece of clothing, you put it on to see whether it fits and looks nice.

12 If you ask someone how they are _____ with an activity, you are asking how they are progressing with it.

13 To _____ someone is to pay them a short visit.

14 If you _____ a particular kind of food, then this is the only kind of food you eat.

15 When a television programme _____, it starts being broadcast.

16 If you _____ someone's mail, you post it on to him or her after you have received it.

(b) *Now complete the following sentences with a suitable phrasal verb with 'on'. Choose from the verbs in exercise (a) and make any changes where necessary.*

1 'What time does *Top of the Pops* _____?'
'At seven, I think. Just after the news.'

2 My son isn't _____ very well in his new school. He's finding the work too hard.

3 'Do you like Chinese food, Paul?'
'Oh yes! I practically _____ it. It's not often I eat anything else.'

4 'Could I _____ the dress in the window, please?'
'I'd prefer you to use the fitting-room, madam.'

5 It must have been standing in the pouring rain watching the match yesterday that _____ your cold.

6 If you could just _____ a moment, please, I'll just see if Mr Collins is free.

7 When I went to work in London for six weeks, I got my sister to _____ my mail.

8 It's dark in here. Someone _____ the light, please.

9 Let's _____ Andy and Lynne tonight. It's ages since we last saw them.

10 If you're still looking for a job, Rose, I hear that Woolworth are _____ extra staff for the sales.

11 You can't _____ working non-stop like that. You've got to take a break some time.

12 I won't let you down, Paula, You know you can _____ me.

13 Do you mean to say that he just _____, without doing anything, when those two men were attacking his brother?

14 Do you think this new fashion will _____?

15 The meeting seemed to _____ for hours, without us really getting anywhere.

16 The other girls at school have been bullying me again. Why do they always _____ me?

Phrasal verbs with 'out'

(a) *Complete the definitions below with a suitable phrasal verb. Choose from the following and make any changes where necessary.*

break out	find out	look out	run out
check out	hand out	make out	stand out
come out	knock out	pass out	try out
die out	leave out	put out	turn out

1 When you shout '_____!' it is to warn someone that they are in danger in some way, for example, when a car is coming towards them and they perhaps don't notice it.

2 If you _____ a fire, you extinguish it.

3 If you _____ something _____, you test it to see that it works, etc.

4 If you _____ something, such as books, you give each person in a group one.

5 If war or an epidemic _____, it starts suddenly and quickly spreads.

6 If a tradition or an animal species _____, it gradually ceases to be practised or exist and eventually disappears.

7 If a factory _____ something, it produces it, usually in large quantities.

8 To _____ means to faint or lose consciousness.

9 When you _____ of a hotel, you pay the bill and return your room key before departing.

10 If something _____, it is very noticeable in some way or other.

11 If you _____ something _____ of a list, group, etc. you do not include it.

12 To _____ something means to learn or discover something that you did not know before, usually by making enquiries.

13 If you can _____ something, you manage to see, read or hear it.

14 When a book _____, it is published or is made available to the public.

15 If a boxer _____ an opponent, he hits him so hard that his opponent loses consciousness for a while or is unable to recover from the blow in time.

16 If a legal document, such as a visa, or a contract _____, it expires and is therefore no longer valid.

(b) *Now complete the following sentences with a suitable phrasal verb with 'out'. Choose from the verbs in exercise (a) and make any changes where necessary.*

1 I'm not exactly sure when the train leaves, but if you wait here I'll try and _____.

2 He was very disappointed when he was _____ of the team for the match against Manchester United.

3 The room was so hot and stuffy that she thought she was going to _____.

4 This factory _____ 2,000 radios every day.

5 She was late _____ of her hotel and almost missed her flight to New York.

6 The boxer won the fight when he _____ his opponent in the fourth round.

7 My passport _____ at the end of the month. I'd better go and renew it next week.

8 Do you mind if I _____ the car _____ before I buy it?

9 World War II _____ in 1939.

10 The teacher asked one of the students to _____ the exam papers.

11 She had bright red hair and really _____ in a crowd.

12 '_____! There's a car coming!' he shouted to the child who was about to cross the road.

13 I see his new novel _____ tomorrow. I hope it's as good as his last one.

14 His handwriting was so bad that I had great difficulty in _____ what he had written.

15 Only about 20 per cent of the population of Wales speak Welsh nowadays. Unless something is done soon, there is a great danger that the language will _____ by the middle of the next century.

16 It took firemen nearly twelve hours to _____ the blaze.

Phrasal verbs with 'up'

(a) Complete the definitions below with a suitable phrasal verb. Choose from the following and make any changes where necessary.

blow up	dress up	– hold up	pull up
cheer up	– go up	make up	put up
– come up	grow up	own up	– slip up
– do up	– hang up	– play up	sum up

1 If you are phoning someone and they _____, they end the phone call, often abruptly, by putting down the receiver.

2 If you _____ to something, you admit that you did it.

3 If you _____ someone _____, you let them stay with you for one or more nights.

4 When you tell someone to _____, you want them to be more mature and to stop behaving in a silly, childish way.

5 When someone _____ after a speech or a debate, they summarize or give the main points of the arguments, etc.

6 If you _____ something _____, such as a building, you destroy it by using explosives.

7 If two people _____, this means they have become friends again after a quarrel.

8 To _____ means to make a mistake.

9 To _____ a building is to repair, modernize or decorate it.

10 If someone, especially a child, _____ you _____, he or she is being naughty and is very difficult to control.

11 If something _____ in a meeting, conversation, etc. it means it is mentioned or discussed.

12 If people _____ a bank, a post office, a security van, etc. they rob it, usually by threatening with weapons.

13 If you tell someone to _____, you want them to stop being depressed and to become happier.

14 If you _____, you put on smart or formal clothes, usually because you are going somewhere special.

15 When a vehicle _____, it slows down then stops.

16 If things _____, for example, prices, it means they rise or increase.

(b) *Now complete the following sentences with a suitable phrasal verb with 'up'. Choose from the verbs in exercise (a) and make any changes where necessary.*

1 Do we really have to _____ for John's party? Can't we just go in jeans?

2 Two armed men _____ a security van early this morning and got away with nearly £300,000.

3 We couldn't believe our eyes when a Rolls-Royce _____ outside the supermarket and the Prime Minister got out.

4 After the debate, the chairman _____ the main points.

5 I do wish he'd _____. I hate miserable people!

6 You're so childish, Simon! Why don't you _____?

7 I think we've _____ somewhere. These sums don't add up properly.

8 The terrorists were caught trying to _____ the Severn Bridge.

9 The nicest thing about quarrelling is _____ afterwards.

10 If you're going to London, don't book into a hotel. My sister will _____ you _____.

11 They bought an old cottage at an auction very cheaply, hoping to _____ it _____ and sell it for a huge profit.

12 'Unless the person who smashed the window _____, none of you will be allowed to go to the school dance on Saturday,' the teacher told her class.

13 I was phoning James, but before I could ask him if he was coming to the party he _____.

14 Did anything interesting _____ at the meeting?

15 This is the third month running that the price of petrol has _____. If this continues, we won't be able to run a car.

16 The children were _____ the new and inexperienced teacher.

Complete the captions 2

Complete the captions in the drawings below using a suitable phrasal verb from the previous three exercises, namely ones with 'on', 'out' and 'up'.

1 He's_____ the books_____.

2 He's_____.

3 She _____
  in the crowd.

4 It will never _____!

5 They're _____.

6 He's _____
  him _____.

7 She's _____
  it _____.

8 They've _____
  the bridge _____.

9 The price has _____.

10 _____!

11 They've _____ it _____ .

12 They're _____ .

13 The meeting is _____
_____ .

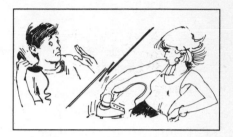

14 She's _____ .

15 It's _____ .

16 They've _____ .

17 The crowd is _____ .

18 She's _____ .

Other useful phrasal verbs

(a) *Complete the definitions below with a suitable phrasal verb. Choose from the following and make any changes where necessary.*

bring round	get through	go with	take away
fall through	go around/round	pass away	take over
get at	go over	pull through	take to
get away	go through	stand for	turn away

1 If you <u>go through</u> something, such as pain, loss, etc. you suffer or experience it.

2 If letters or initials <u>stand for</u> something, for example, BBC, they are an abbreviation for the whole word or name.

3 If you <u>take to</u> someone or something, you begin to form a liking for them.

4 If you <u>bring</u> someone <u>round</u>, you revive them or make them conscious again after they have been unconscious.

5 If you <u>get through</u> to someone, you manage to contact them by telephone.

6 If someone <u>pulls through</u>, they manage to recover from a serious illness or accident.

7 If you <u>turn</u> someone <u>away</u>, you refuse to allow them to enter a building, such as a nightclub, disco, etc.

8 If plans or arrangements <u>fall through</u>, they fail to materialize in some way and have to be abandoned.

9 If you <u>go over</u> something, you examine or check it carefully.

10 If you <u>take away</u> one number from another, you subtract the one from the other.

11 If something <u>goes with</u> something else, then it matches it in some way.

12 If something is difficult to <u>get at</u>, it means it is difficult to reach.

13 If one company _takes over_ another, then it gains control of it financially.

14 If there is enough of something to _go round_, for example, some sweets, then there is enough for everyone in the group to have a share.

15 If you _get away_ from somewhere or someone, you manage to escape.

16 If someone has _pass away_, this means they have died.

(b) *Now complete the following sentences with a suitable phrasal verb from the ones in exercise (a). Make any changes where necessary.*

1 His injuries after the car accident were so serious that doctors didn't think he'd _pull through_.

2 Many smaller companies run the risk of being _taken over_ by larger ones.

3 Share these sandwiches among you. There should be enough to _go round_.

4 The doorman at the Green Man nightclub _turned_ us _away_ because we were wearing jeans and leather jackets.

5 'Do you have any curtains that will _go with_ a green carpet?' he asked the shop assistant.

6 Our plans to hold an open-air pop concert _turned down_ / _fell through_ when local residents objected to it.

7 He tried playing golf once but never really _took to_ it. It was too slow and he found he had to walk too much.

8 Poor Susan. She's really _going through_ a lot this year, what with first losing her job, and now the death of her mother.

9 'What do you get if you _take away_ 17 from 94?'
'Seventy-seven.'

10 The pickpocket was caught, but then managed to _get away_ by running through the crowd.

115

11 'Julia's fainted!'

'Well, throw some water on her face. That should __bring__ her __round__.'

12 The old lady finally _passed away_ at the weekend. She was 94 and had been ill for some time.

13 Make sure you put the tablets on the top shelf of the cupboard so that the children can't _get at_ them.

14 'What do the letters UNESCO _stands for_?'

'I'm not sure. Something to do with the United Nations, I think.'

15 I think we'd better _go over_ the accounts again, just to make sure we haven't made any mistakes.

16 I tried phoning the BBC after the programme to protest, but couldn't _get through_. All the lines were engaged.

Three-part phrasal verbs 1

Complete the phrases 1–12 with a suitable ending a–l. Write your answers in the boxes on the opposite page.

1 I'd signed the contract, so it was too late to

2 You go along now. I'll

3 They should *do away with*

4 Don't let him bully you, try to

5 It's about time we

6 He *went back on*

7 This house

8 Children often bite their nails

9 The musical didn't really

a *got down to* some serious work.

b but they soon *grow out of* it.

c the summer holidays.

d *back out of* the deal.

e *live up to* her expectations.

f your offer.

g these silly rules.

h his promise.

i *catch up with* you later.

j *stand up to* him.

k *goes back to* 1789.

l *fit in with* the others in the group.

10 We're *looking forward to*

11 She didn't really

12 I'd like to *take you up on*

1	2	3	4	5	6	7	8	9	10	11	12
D	I	G	J	A	C	K	B	E	H	L	F

Three-part phrasal verbs 2

Complete the phrases 1–12 with suitable endings a–l. Write your answers in the boxes on the next page.

1 When they *checked up on* her,

2 It was the first time they'd ever

3 They *came up with*

4 We didn't *feel up to*

5 He isn't old,

6 Since I'd promised, I couldn't

7 Sally can't come. She's

8 I think I'll *go in for*

9 Although the course was difficult, he still

10 I always listen to the news to

a *get out of* it.

b *went through with* it.

c *run out of* peas.

d the Cambridge Proficiency examination next year.

e they found she had a prison record.

f *keep up with* what's going on in the world.

g lots of new ideas.

h *gone down with* measles.

i *come up against* such a problem.

j but he must be *getting on for* forty-five.

k doing anything energetic.

11 She's a real snob and
12 Would you like cabbage instead, as we've

1 *looks down on* anyone who is poor or working-class.

1	2	3	4	5	6	7	8	9	10	11	12

Nouns from phrasal verbs 1

Fill in the missing nouns in the sentences below. Choose from the following:

break-in	downpour	kick-off	outcome
breakdown	flashback	lay-by	output
by-pass	get-together	let-down	setback
check-up	handout	mix-up	take-off
comeback	hold-up	onset	turnover

1 There was an hour's _____ on the Underground this morning owing to a power failure on the Central Line.

2 The final _____ of the election is not yet known, but it looks like the Labour party has been defeated again.

3 This company has an annual _____ of nearly £600 million.

4 I think I'll have to get my car seen to. This is the fourth _____ I've had this month.

5 We're having a little _____ at the weekend to celebrate the end of term. Would you like to come?

6 Owing to a _____, I was put into a smoking compart-
ment on the train rather than a non-smoking one.

7 Despite this early _____, we're confident that we shall
complete the project on time.

8 This is the third _____ in Grove Road this week. Police
are warning residents to make sure all doors and windows are
locked.

9 A sudden _____ delayed the start of the Wimbledon
men's singles final for over an hour.

10 The 'dream holiday' they had advertised was a total waste of
money. What a _____!

11 I enjoy flying, but I still get a bit nervous during the
_____ and the landing.

12 'The scene starts with James staring at a photo of Alice. Then
we get a quick _____ to the time they first met,' the
director explained.

13 He went to the doctor for his annual _____.

14 She had been driving for several hours, so she decided to pull
into a _____ for a rest.

15 Lots of pop groups from the seventies and eighties have been
trying to make a _____ recently.

16 Tottenham Hotspur took the lead with a brilliant goal just
minutes after the _____.

17 Traffic jams in the town centre are very rare since they built the
new _____.

18 The _____ of the disease is marked by a high fever and a
feeling of giddiness.

19 Each student got a _____ on phrasal verbs to study for
homework.

20 The _____ from this factory is slowly increasing. By the
end of the year we hope to be producing 2,000 computers a
week.

Nouns from phrasal verbs 2

Fill in the missing nouns in the sentences below. Choose from the following:

> → *situation which is poor and unpleasant, after one has been used too smthg much better.*

break-up	follow-up	layout	stop-over
breakthrough	getaway	lookout	turnout
come-down	grown-ups	onlookers	upkeep
cutbacks	intake	outbreak	write-off
drawbacks	knockout	outlook	write-up

disadvantage *bloqueado* *future.*

1 The _____ for the future is brighter now than it has been for many years.

2 They had to sell the house because the _____ was too expensive.

3 The Art College was very popular, with an average ___*intake*___ each year of about 300 students.

4 One of the main _____ of living in Wales is that it's a bit too far from London.

5 The film got a very good _____ in today's papers. The critics must have liked it very much.

6 Many people blame the tabloid newspapers for the _____ of the marriage of Prince Charles and Princess Diana.

7 The architect went over the _____ of the new office block with the managing director.

8 We're expecting a huge _____ for tomorrow's open-air concert in Hyde Park.

9 He considered the splitting of the atom to be the major scientific _____ of the century.

10 The party is for _____ only. No children are allowed.

11 Further _____ in public spending are necessary to bring Government borrowing down.

12 He escaped uninjured in the accident, but his car was a complete _____ .

13 A crowd of _____ gathered to watch the latest episode of the TV soap *Eastenders* being made.

14 From being a prominent government minister it was quite a _____ for him to be just an ordinary member of parliament.

15 The robbers escaped before the police could catch them, when they were warned by one of the gang who was acting as a _____ .

16 This year's conference in Swansea is a _____ to the one we had last year in Bournemouth.

17 This is the third _____ of cholera in the region in the past year.

18 The champion won by a _____ in the third round.

19 Our trip to Australia included a three-day _____ in Singapore.

20 After the robbery, the thieves made their _____ in a stolen police car.

Follow up: Phrasal verb quiz

Work in pairs or groups of three. Read through the following questions and write your answers on a separate piece of paper. (The nouns and phrasal verbs used are the ones found in the previous five exercises.)

1 Name two things that can **fall through**.
2 They were **turned away**. What happened to them?
3 Where would you normally go for a **check-up**?
4 Name three important **breakthroughs** in science, medicine or technology this century.
5 What sort of things can cause the **break-up** of a marriage?
6 If you had a pink sofa, which colour curtains and carpet would **go with** it?

7 How would you feel if you found out that someone had been **checking up on** you?

8 If you saw the headline CHAMP WINS BY **KNOCKOUT** in the newspaper, which sport would this be?

9 Why was he happy when he was told that his wife would **pull through**?

10 What does 'NASA' **stand for**?

11 Which diseases do children often **go down with**?

12 Name at least two things you have **grown out of**.

13 What does it mean if you are told that your car is a **write-off**?

14 Where might you find a **by-pass**?

15 Name three things you are **looking forward to**.

16 Why did she cry when she heard that her friend had **passed away**?

17 Name someone or something that has made a successful **comeback**.

18 Name something that you haven't **got round to** doing yet.

19 What might you get a good or a bad **write-up** for?

20 What are the **drawbacks**, if any, of being (a) a woman (b) a man?

21 Who might you phone if you had a **break-in**?

22 What could you do to try to **bring** someone **round**?

23 Name any film you have seen or book you have read that hasn't **lived up to** your expectations.

24 Has anything ever been a **let-down**? What?

When you have finished, compare your answers with another pair or group in the class.

In other words...

(a) Match the situations 1–10 with suitable idioms, a–j. Write your answers in the boxes on the next page.

1 'I spend more than I earn. What am I going to do?'

2 She told everyone about the wedding. It was supposed to be a secret.

3 She's unemployed and is receiving money from the government until she finds a new job.

4 She was feeling very restless.

5 He tricked her out of £5,000.

6 She's very musical – just like her mother.

7 'I can't stop the baby crying. I've tried every-thing. I just don't know what to do next!'

8 'That's the last time I go ice-skating. My body's full of bruises.'

9 She's very good at gardening.

10 Doreen is looking after the shop while Mary is at lunch.

a She was like a cat on hot bricks.

b She's at the end of her tether.

c She's holding the fort.

d She can't make ends meet.

e She's black and blue all over.

f She's on the dole.

g She's got green fingers.

h She's been taken for a ride.

i She let the cat out of the bag.

j She's a chip off the old block.

1	2	3	4	5	6	7	8	9	10

(b) Now complete the following six dialogues with suitable idioms. Choose from the above list and make any necessary changes.

1 A: My garden's such a mess!

    B: Well, Paul's got _____. Maybe he could help you.

2 A: How long has Paula been _____?

    B: About five months now. Between you and me I don't think she'll ever get a job again. She's too old.

3 A: I hear Dave was _____ last week.

    B: What do you mean?

    A: Well, apparently he was offered a Jaguar for £1,000. It turned out it was stolen. So now he's lost both the car and his money.

4 A: Things are so expensive these days.

    B: You're telling me! If both John and I weren't working I really don't know how we'd _____.

5 A: That's the first and last time I ever play rugby!

    B: Didn't you like it, then?

    A: Not a bit. I was covered in mud and _____. I ached for a week afterwards.

6 A: Could you _____ please, Julie, while I pop down to the bank?

    B: Yes, of course.

124

Section Five: Idioms 1

Idioms using adjectives

Fill in the missing adjectives in the definitions below. Choose from the following:

brainy	hard up	stony broke
browned-off	hot-headed	thick-skinned
cheeky	ill at ease	tight-fisted
dead beat	long-winded	tongue-tied
dog-eared	nosy	two-faced
down-at-heel	pig-headed	well-off
hair-raising	single-handed	

1 If you are _____, you are very inquisitive, especially about other people, and interested in things that are not really any of your business.

2 If you are _____, you are very insensitive to criticism or blame, especially when directed to yourself, and consequently are not easily offended.

3 If you are _____, you are rich or wealthy.

4 If you are _____, you are fed up, bored or irritated by something.

5 If you are _____, you tend to do things without thinking and also get angry very quickly.

6 If you do something _____, you do it alone, without anyone else's help.

7 If you are _____, you are very intelligent and usually good at studying.

8 If you are _____, you are too shy or nervous to speak, especially because you feel awkward in front of other people.

9 If you are _____, you feel awkward, nervous and uneasy in the presence of others.

10 If you are _____, you look poor, untidy and your clothes are shabby and worn-out.

11 If you are _____, you are very mean with money and hate spending it unnecessarily.

12 If you are _____, you are short of money, whereas if you are _____, you don't have any money at all.

13 If you are _____, you agree with a person when talking to him but disagree with him behind his back. In other words, you are deceitful and insincere.

14 If a book is _____, the corners of the pages have been folded down, usually because it has been read a lot.

15 If a speech is _____, it is usually boring and goes on far too long.

16 Children who are _____ are very rude, impolite or disrespectful, especially towards those who are older than themselves, such as teachers, their parents, etc.

17 Something that is _____ is very frightening.

18 If you are _____, you are very stubborn and unwilling to listen to advice or to change your mind.

19 If you are _____, you are feeling very tired or exhausted.

Idioms using nouns

Fill in the missing nouns in the definitions below. Choose from the following:

backlash	catcall	hallmark	racket
bloodbath	eye-opener	heyday	scapegoat
blow	figurehead	loophole	skinflint
bottleneck	gimmick	nest egg	snag
brainwave	godsend	nickname	windfall

1 If there is a _____ in, for example, a tax law, this means there is a way of escaping or avoiding paying tax quite legally because the actual wording of the law has not been written carefully enough.

2 A _____ is someone who is unfairly blamed or punished for the mistakes of others, usually because people are very angry and want to see someone blamed or punished.

3 A _____ is a sum of money that you get unexpectedly, such as winning the football pools or a lottery, etc.

4 A _____ is someone who is the leader of a country or organization, but in name only. He or she doesn't have any real power.

5 If you say that something, for example, a painting has the _____ of a certain artist, you mean that it has the typical features or qualities of a painting by that particular artist.

6 A _____ is a sudden angry or violent reaction by a group of people against the actions or decisions of others, especially the government, the police or others in authority.

7 If you have a _____, you have a sudden, very clear idea.

8 A _____ is someone who is mean and miserly and hates spending or giving money away.

9 If an event is described as a _____, this means that a lot of people were killed at one time, usually violently.

10 If something is an _____, you find it very surprising and, in the process, you also learn something from it which you did not know before.

11 A _____ is an informal name usually used by family and friends, and is often connected with a person's character or physical characteristics. So a fat person might be called 'Tubby' or a tall person 'Lofty', etc.

12 A _____ is a small, often hidden or unexpected, problem or disadvantage.

13 A _____ is a disappointment or a piece of bad news.

14 A _____ is some sort of trick, device or unusual action whose purpose is to attract attention or publicity, usually when trying to sell something to people.

15 If people are making a _____, they are making a very loud, unpleasant noise.

16 A _____ is a narrow part of a street which slows down traffic, thus often causing long delays.

17 A _____ is something, possibly unexpected, which is badly needed and, therefore, very useful such as getting a legacy when you are short of money.

18 A _____ is a loud whistle or cry of disapproval from, for example, an audience at a theatre or a crowd at a football match.

19 A person, country or organization's _____ is the time when they were most powerful, successful or popular.

20 A _____ is an amount of money that you save for use some time in the future, such as when you get married, retire, etc.

Idioms using adjectives and nouns

Fill in the missing words in the definitions below. Choose from the following.

blue-eyed boy	mixed blessing	stiff upper lip
confirmed bachelor	practical joke	sweeping statement
dead heat	raw deal	tall order
double Dutch	red tape	tight spot
general dogsbody	short cut	vicious circle
golden handshake	sore point	wishful thinking
last straw	spitting image	

1 If you take a _____ to a place, you find a quicker or easier way to get there.

2 A _____ is a wide generalization, such as 'all Welsh people can sing', 'all black people are good at dancing', etc.

3 If prices rise, workers ask for higher wages. If they get higher wages, prices rise. A situation like this, where cause and effect follow each other continually is often referred to as a _____.

4 If you are given a _____, you get a large payment when you leave a company, especially when the company has asked you to leave.

5 If a student is a teacher's _____ then he is that teacher's favourite student.

6 If you play a _____ on someone, you play a trick on them, usually in order to amuse others.

7 If you say that someone is the _____ of another person, you mean that they look very much like that other person.

8 _____ is when you imagine that something is true or will happen simply because you want it to be so. In reality, it is very unlikely to happen or be true.

9 If a man is a _____ he is very unlikely ever to get married.

10 If you keep a _____, you don't show any emotion or appear upset when hearing a piece of bad news or suffering bad luck.

11 If you describe something as the _____, it is an additional problem or difficulty in a series of unpleasant events that makes you feel that you have reached breaking point and just can't take any more.

12 If you say that something you have heard or read is _____ to you, you mean that it was either difficult to understand, meaningless or nonsense.

13 If you find yourself in a _____, you are in a difficult or dangerous situation.

14 If something is a _____ with you, it is likely to upset you or make you angry if someone tries to discuss it with you.

15 If you are the _____ in an office, you do all the boring, routine and mechanical jobs there, usually the jobs no one else wants to do.

16 If you say that a task you have been given is a _____, you mean that it will be very difficult to accomplish.

17 If you have been given a _____, you have been treated unfairly in some way.

18 If you say that a situation is a _____, you mean that it has many advantages but also lots of disadvantages too.

19 A _____ is a race in which two people finish at exactly the same time.

20 When there are too many official rules and regulations, especially in Government departments, which often seem unnecessary and nearly always cause delays, these are generally referred to as too much _____.

Idioms using noun phrases

Fill in the missing noun phrases in the definitions below. Choose from the following:

a blessing in disguise	the odd man out
chicken-feed	the pros and cons
child's play	the rat race
a drop in the ocean	a shot in the dark
elbow grease	a sight for sore eyes
a flash in the pan	a slip of the tongue
a fly in the ointment	a stick-in-the-mud
the gift of the gab	a stone's throw
a jack-of-all-trades	a storm in a teacup
the life and soul of the party	teething troubles

1 If you describe someone as _____, you mean that they are very lively, laugh and joke a lot and generally provide fun for others.

2 _____ is a wild, random guess which is unlikely to be successful.

3 If you call someone _____, you mean that they are very stubborn and conservative and don't like trying out anything new.

4 _____ is a small problem or other minor incident that spoils something that is otherwise perfect or satisfactory.

5 If you say that something is _____, you mean that it caused problems and difficulties at first, but later on you realized that it was the best thing that could have happened.

6 When you weigh up _____ of a proposal, you carefully consider the arguments for and against it.

7 If a situation is described as _____, it means that a lot of fuss and excitement is being made about something that is not really important.

8 If someone is suddenly successful or popular, but their success or popularity only lasts a short time and is never repeated, then that person can be described as _____ .

9 If you say that someone or something is _____ , you mean that the person or thing is a very pleasant and welcome sight.

10 When you describe a sum of money as _____ , you mean that it is a very small, unimportant amount of money.

11 The project had _____ . This means it had problems or difficulties in the early stages of it.

12 If you say that one place is only _____ from another, you mean that they are only a short distance from each other.

13 If you have _____ , you are able to speak fluently, confidently and very persuasively.

14 If you describe a task as _____ , you mean that it is very easy to do.

15 When you say that someone or something is _____ , you mean that the person or thing is different in some way from the others in a group.

16 If you put some _____ into your work, you use more energy or muscle strength, especially when polishing or cleaning.

17 If you decide to opt out of _____ , you decide to leave a way of life in which you were always competing with others in a bitter struggle for social status and success in your job.

18 If you are _____ , you can do many different kinds of jobs, such as painting and decorating, repairing a car, gardening, etc. though you may not be an expert in any of them.

19 If you are £70,000 in debt and a friend offers to help you by giving you £500, this sum can be described as _____ since it is only a fraction of what is needed.

20 If you make a careless mistake when speaking, such as pronouncing a word incorrectly or saying something that you didn't really mean to say, this is known as _____ .

Paired idioms

Complete the paired idioms in the sentences below with the correct word. Choose from the following.

bright	downs	live	square
bustle	dried	scrimp	sweet
buts	games	see	touch
change	give	sick	turn
choose	later	sound	wear

1 As soon as the teacher left the classroom, the children got up to all sorts of *fun and* _____.

2 She was so relieved when her son phoned to say that he was *safe and* _____. She was worried that he'd been killed in the train crash she'd heard about on the news.

3 This carpet is made from special fibres and should stand a lot of _____ *and tear*.

4 Life is full of *ups and* _____. You just hope you get more good times than bad ones.

5 My father's a milkman and has to get up _____ *and early* every morning.

6 The Swedish tennis team were beaten *fair and* _____ by Australia in the final of the Davis Cup.

7 I haven't told my parents yet that I'm thinking of taking a job in London. They won't like it I know, but I've got to leave home *sooner or* _____.

8 He moved to the country, but before long he found he was missing the *hustle and* _____ of city life.

9 He suffered from insomnia and would *toss and* _____ for hours each night before he finally managed to fall asleep.

10 I wish your brother wouldn't *chop and* _____ his plans all the time. I wish he'd make up his mind once and for all.

11 Her husband was in a very critical condition after the accident. In fact it was _____ *and go* whether he would pull through.

12 With your qualifications and experience you ought to be able to *pick and* _____ any job you want.

13 A certain amount of _____ *and take* is necessary in all marriages.

14 If we buy a house we'll probably have to _____ *and save* for the next twenty years.

15 I don't want any *ifs and* _____, just make sure you hand in the homework tomorrow.

16 It's too early yet to say whether the group's first record will be a hit or not. We'll just have to *wait and* _____.

17 The result of tomorrow's by-election is more or less *cut and* _____. I will be very surprised if the Labour Party loses.

18 He was _____ *and tired* of people patting his head and saying how bald he was getting.

19 I didn't bother to lock the back door when I popped down to the local shop. When I returned, my stereo and TV had been stolen! Well, you _____ *and learn*, don't you? I'll never go out again without locking every door.

20 The only thing I remember about my wedding was that the ceremony was *short and* _____. It couldn't have lasted more than ten minutes.

Complete the captions

Complete the captions in the drawings below with a suitable idiom. Choose from the idioms using adjectives and nouns, and idioms using noun phrases on pages 129–132.

1 She's the _____
_____ .

2 It's a _____ .

3 He's got the _____
_____ .

4 It's _____
to her.

5 They're taking a _____
_____ to the station.

6 The dog on the left is the
_____ .

7 They were just a _____
_____ .

8 It sounds like _____
_____ to him.

9 He's a _____ .

10 She's the _____
_____ in our office.

11 It's a _____ .

12 He's the _____
of his father.

Read and discuss

Work in pairs of groups of three. Read through the following and take it in turns to give your answers. (The idioms are the ones found on pages 125–134.)

1 Have you ever felt **browned off**? If so, explain what caused it and what happened.

2 Do you or anyone you know have a **nickname**? What is it? How did you or they get it?

3 Which would you prefer to be – **brainy** or good-looking? Give reasons for your choice.

4 Can you think of any **gimmicks** you have seen or read about that companies use to sell products? *(For example, free glasses or other presents when you buy petrol.)*

5 If you were a parent and you found out that your children had been **cheeky**, would you punish them? If so, how? If not, why not?

6 If you could **pick and choose** any job in the world, what job would you choose and why?

7 What's the most **hair-raising** thing that's ever happened to you?

8 Do you understand why some men are **confirmed bachelors**? What are the advantages and disadvantages of never getting married?

9 Do you ever feel **ill at ease** or **tongue-tied** in front of people? If so, what was the occasion and how did you cope? If not, why do you think some people feel like this?

10 Have you ever played a **practical joke** on anyone or had one played on you? If so, describe it.

11 Some people sail **single-handed** around the world. What other thngs like this have you heard of people doing single-handed?

12 Is there a lot of **red tape** in your country? Give some examples of things that can take a long time to do because of bureaucracy.

13 Who is the **nosiest** person you have ever met? Give examples to show how 'nosy' this person was.

14 If you could be the **spitting image** of anyone, who would you choose to be and why?

15 What sort of **fun and games** did you used to get up to when you were younger?

16 When was the last time you got up **bright and early**? Why? Where were you going?

17 How much do you have to earn a year in your country to be considered **well-off**?

18 Have you or someone you know ever been in a **tight spot**? If so, describe what happened.

19 Is a typical person in your country **hot-headed**? What in general terms are the main characteristics of people in your country? *(hard-working, shy, friendly, etc.)*

20 'British people always talk about the weather.' This is a rather **sweeping statement** as there are many British people who never talk about the weather. Think up some sweeping statements of your own about (a) women (b) men (c) politicians (d) teachers (e) another nationality *(French people..., Spanish people... etc.)*

Idioms using prepositions 1

Fill in the missing idioms from the sentences below. Choose from the following and make any necessary changes to the words in italics.

above board	in deep water	on the tip of *one's*
at a loose end	in the flesh	tongue
at random	in the nick of time	out of *one's* depth
behind bars	off the top of *one's*	out of order
by chance	head	out of tune
for good	on fire	up in arms
in a flash	on the air	
in a nutshell	on the house	

1 If you see someone in reality rather than in a photograph or on television, then you can say that you have seen the person _____.

2 The Prime Minister is making a broadcast to the nation on television tonight. He will be _____ at nine o'clock.

3 The lift was broken, so it had a sign on the door saying '_____'.

4 If you meet someone _____, you meet them accidentally or unexpectedly. You didn't plan it.

5 If a business activity is honest and legal, then you can describe it as being _____.

6 If you don't have time to think or prepare something, for example, the answer to a question you are asked, you may have to give an answer _____.

7 If you are _____ about something, you are very angry about it or protesting strongly about it.

8 If you explain something _____, you give a very brief and concise explanation of it.

9 If you find you have nothing to do this weekend, you can say that you're _____ this weekend.

10 If you are about to say a person's name but just for the moment can't quite remember it, you can say that it's _____.

11 If there is a fire and the fire brigade arrive _____, they arrive just in time to put it out. If they had arrived any later, it would have been too late.

12 If you choose something _____, you choose it by chance, without making a deliberate choice.

13 We couldn't play the piano because it sounded dreadful. None of the notes were right. It was really _____.

14 They called the fire brigade because their house was _____.

15 If someone is _____, they are in a serious situation or in serious trouble.

16 If a hotel manager tells his guests that the drinks are _____, it means they are free.

17 I called for an ambulance and it arrived here almost immediately. It was here _____.

18 He spent twenty years _____, that is, in prison.

19 If you leave your country permanently and don't ever intend returning, you can say that you are leaving your country _____.

20 If you go on a course and find it much too difficult, you can say that you were _____.

Idioms using prepositions 2

Fill in the missing idioms in the sentences below. Choose from the following and make any necessary changes to the words in italics.

at loggerheads	in a rut	on the dot
at short notice	in stitches	out of print
at will	in the limelight	out of the question
by ear	in vain	out of this world
down the drain	on average	over the moon
for the time being	on *one's* last legs	up *someone's* street
from scratch	on purpose	

1 If you broke a window _____, it means you did it deliberately. It was no accident.

2 She was extremely happy when she heard she had got the job. She was _____.

3 If you learn something _____, for example a language, it means you're a complete beginner when you start the course and have no previous knowledge of the language.

4 If you are asked to work overtime _____, it means you are given very little warning in advance.

5 Pop stars and film-stars are always _____. They are always in the public eye and the centre of attention.

6 Gambling is something I like and am good at. It's right _____.

7 The old man was very weak and was close to death. He was _____.

8 If you have to live for a short while in a hotel while you're looking for a house to buy, you can say that you're living in a hotel _____.

9 If two people are having a disagreement or quarrel about something, you can say that they're _____.

10 Some teachers here work only 12 hours a week, others work 22 hours and some 26 hours. But _____ they work about 20 hours a week.

11 She wanted to borrow my car for the weekend. I told her it wasn't possible – it was quite _____.

12 He wasted £80 betting on horses, because he didn't win anything. It was £80 _____!

13 If you have to be somewhere at exactly seven-thirty, then you can say that you have to be there at seven thirty _____.

14 The food at this restaurant is absolutely marvellous. It's _____!

15 When she told us the joke about the teacher and the octopus we were _____. We just couldn't stop laughing.

16 A chameleon is able to change the colour of its skin whenever it wants to. In other words, it can change the colour of its skin _____.

17 If a book is _____, you can no longer buy a new copy of it, but you might be able to find an old copy in a second-hand book shop.

18 He tried _____ to pass his driving test. In other words, he tried but wasn't successful.

19 He couldn't read music. He played the piano _____ instead.

20 If you find you are leading the sort of life where your job and everything else has become very routine and boring, with no chance of changing anything, then you might feel that you were _____.

Follow up

Complete the following sentences with a suitable idiom. Choose from the ones in the previous two exercises.

1 'I saw the Prime Minister yesterday.'
   'What, on TV?'
   'No, _____! He was standing as close to me as you are now.'

2 That was no accident, Nick. You dropped the vase we got from Aunt Mary _____. I saw you!

3 If you're _____ on Friday evening, why not come round to my place? We can have a meal and a chat.

4 I'm sorry, but you can't go on holiday with Mandy and Julie. It's quite _____. You're all far too young to go abroad on your own.

5 Don't forget – the train leaves at 8 o'clock _____. So you'd better not be late!

6 You can't expect me to arrange a board meeting _____ such _____. I need at least a week to contact everyone.

7 'I see her husband's _____ again.'
   'What for this time?'
   'Armed robbery, I think.'

8 Congratulations, madam! You're the ten thousandth customer at our restaurant, so tonight's meal won't cost you a penny – it's _____!

9 'Have you got a copy of *Savage Winds* by I. C. Fields?'
   'Sorry, it's _____. But there's a second-hand bookshop round the corner. They might have a copy.'

10 The comedian was really funny and had the whole audience
_____.

11 When you play bingo, the numbers are called out _____,
so you never know which number will come up next.

12 The course was far too difficult for me. I was completely
_____.

In other words...

(a) *Match the situations 1–10 with a suitable idiom a–j. Write your
answers in the boxes on the next page.*

1 Write to me some time.

2 Hurry up!

3 It's a secret, so don't tell anyone.

4 Calm down! Don't get angry!

5 Don't forget to be on your best behaviour at Aunt Mildred's.

6 The company's £3 million in debt, so they've closed the factory.

7 Would you please come to the point!

8 I was so surprised!

9 If you think I did it, then you're wrong.

10 My house is miles away from anywhere.

a Keep your hair on!

b You could have knocked me down with a feather!

c Drop me a line.

d It's off the beaten track.

e It's gone bust.

f Get a move on!

g You're barking up the wrong tree.

h Mind your p's and q's.

i Keep it under your hat.

j Stop beating about the bush!

1	2	3	4	5	6	7	8	9	10

(b) Now complete the following six dialogues with a suitable idiom. Choose from the above list and make any necessary changes.

1 A: Does Kate live near the town centre?
   B: Oh no, she's got an old cottage in the country. It's really
     _____ – miles from anywhere.

2 A: Come on, you lot! _____! It's nearly nine-thirty. The
     taxi's here!
   B: All right, dad. _____! We're coming!

3 A: It's like this, John. I... I... er, well, how can I put it?
   B: For goodness' sake, _____, Peter! Just tell me, will
     you? I haven't got all day, you know.

4 A: I suppose you heard about Mike winning that talent contest?
   B: Yes. Honestly, _____! I didn't even know he could
     sing.
   A: Neither did I. It was quite a surprise to us all.

5 A: Don't forget to _____ to let me know what
     Australia's like.
   B: It's the first thing I'll do when I get there, I promise.

6 A: Paul and Mary have just got engaged.
   B: Have they really? That's a surprise!
   A: Well, they don't want to tell anyone else yet, so _____.
   B: Don't worry. I won't tell a soul.

Section Six: Idioms 2

Idioms using animals

Fill in the missing idioms in the definitions below. Choose from the following and make any necessary changes, especially to verbs and the words in italics.

as the crow flies
cock-and-bull story
cook someone's goose
donkey's years
flog a dead horse
go to the dogs
get butterflies in *one's* stomach
have a bee in *one's* bonnet
have a whale of a time
hen party
hold your horses

kill two birds with one stone
let sleeping dogs lie
make a pig of *oneself*
no room to swing a cat
put the cat among the pigeons
smell a rat
stag party
straight from the horse's mouth
take the bull by the horns

1 An example of _____ is if you were going to a place on holiday but could, at the same time, carry out some business there.

2 If you _____, you say or do something which provokes quarrelling or argument.

3 If you try to persuade someone, for example, to vote for a particular political party when this person has made it quite clear to you that they are not interested in voting for that party, then you are probably _____. In other words, your efforts are doomed to failure.

145

4 If you are invited to a party and _____, this means you eat or drink too much, usually because you are greedy.

5 If you _____, you decide to face or deal with a difficulty or problem instead of avoiding it.

6 If you _____ before an important event, such as an exam, an interview, etc, it means you feel very nervous.

7 The distance from one place to another _____, is the distance in a straight line. It is usually shorter than the distance measured by road.

8 If you tell someone that there's _____ in your office, you mean that the office is very small and cramped.

9 If you _____ about something, you are obsessed by it and think about it or talk about it all the time.

10 If you _____, you spoil their plans or ruin their chances of success, often intentionally.

11 If you _____, you suspect that something is wrong or become very suspicious about someone or something.

12 Just before two people get married in Britain it is customary for the bride-to-be and her female friends to get together for an evening out. This is usually known as a _____. A similar gathering for the groom-to-be and his male friends is called a _____.

13 If someone told you he was late because he had been captured by aliens and taken aboard a UFO on his way to work, then you would probably think he was telling you a _____.

14 If you get a piece of information _____, you get it directly from a very reliable source, so it is almost certain to be true.

15 If you say '_____!' to someone, you want them to wait a moment and not be in such a hurry to do something.

16 If you haven't seen someone for _____, this means you haven't seen them for a very long time.

17 If you _____ at a party, you really enjoy yourself.

18 The proverb '_____' means that you should not look for trouble but should instead leave things well alone.

19 If someone has _____, they have slowly become ruined both physically and morally, usually through their own fault.

Idioms using colours

Fill in the missing idioms in the definitions below. Choose from the following:

black market	once in a blue moon
blackleg	paint the town red
get the green light	red herring
give someone a black look	red-letter day
green	see red
green belt	tickled pink
grey matter	white elephant
in black and white	white-collar worker
in the red	whitewash
off colour	with flying colours

1 If your bank account is _____, it means that you owe the bank money – in other words you are in debt.

2 A _____ is a very important or joyful occasion in your life, for example, a special birthday, your 25th wedding anniversary, etc.

3 If you try to _____ something, you try to make it appear better than it is by covering up any faults or by attempting to hide any unpleasant facts.

4 In most countries, goods that are scarce or illegal can usually be obtained on the _____, if you have the money to pay for them.

5 If you do something _____, it means you do it very rarely.

6 A _____ is, for example, an office worker rather than a manual worker or factory worker.

7 If you _____, you look angrily at them.

8 If you pass an exam _____, it means you pass it very successfully and with ease.

9 If you are a _____, you continue to work when your fellow-workers are on strike.

10 If you introduce a _____ into a discussion, you deliberately introduce a fact or subject in order to draw attention away from the important matter which is being discussed.

11 Something that costs a lot but is useless is known as a _____.

12 A _____ is an area of fields and woodland around a town or city.

13 If you _____, you celebrate noisily and wildly, often by going to bars, nightclubs, etc.

14 If you _____, you are given permission to go ahead with a plan or a project.

15 If you _____, you suddenly become very angry.

16 When you say that someone doesn't have much _____, you mean that they don't have much intelligence.

17 If you say that someone is _____, you mean that they are new, naïve or inexperienced.

18 If you're _____ with something, you are very pleased with it.

19 If you see or have something _____, it means you see or have it in writing or in print.

20 If you are feeling _____, you are feeling slightly ill.

Idioms using parts of the body

Fill in the missing idioms in the definitions below. Choose from the following and make any necessary changes, especially to verbs and the words in italics.

get cold feet	lose face
get off on the wrong foot	lose one's head
get something off *one's* chest	pay through the nose
have *one's* back to the wall	set *one's* heart on (something)
have *one's* heart in *one's* mouth	stick *one's* neck out
	stretch *one's* legs
have something on the brain	take to *one's* heels
jump down someone's throat	tongue-in-cheek
jump out of *one's* skin	turn a blind eye to (something)
keep *one's* fingers crossed	wet behind the ears
live from hand to mouth	

1 If you _____, you speak angrily to them.

2 If you _____ something, you want it very much.

3 If someone says you're _____, they mean that you're young and inexperienced.

4 If you _____, you suddenly stop something or withdraw from it because you become nervous or frightened of the consequences. For example, you decide not to take a job you've been offered abroad because you're nervous or frightened to leave your country and friends.

5 If you _____, you panic and lose control.

6 If you _____, you run away.

7 If you _____, you feel very nervous or frightened about something.

8 If you _____ something, you deliberately ignore it and pretend that you don't see it.

9 If two people _____, they start their relationship badly.

10 If you _____, you live very poorly, spending any money you earn as soon as you get it, and never being able to save for the future.

11 If you _____, you take a risk, especially by doing or saying something which may cause trouble for yourself. It also means making a prediction which may turn out to be completely wrong.

12 If someone made a sudden, loud noise behind you, you might _____. In other words, you would get a sudden shock or fright.

13 If you say something _____, you don't really mean what you say or expect your words to be taken seriously.

14 If you tell a friend that you will _____ for him, you mean that you hope he will be lucky or successful, for example, in an examination or job interview.

15 If you _____, you finally talk about something that has been bothering you for a long time but which you haven't wanted to talk about until now.

16 If you _____ for something, you pay far more for it than it is really worth.

17 If you _____, for example, golf – it means that you think about it and talk about it all the time.

18 If you _____, you are either made to look foolish or you lose the respect of others.

19 If you _____, you find yourself in a position where you are forced to defend yourself.

20 If you _____, you go for a walk, often after having been sitting down for a long time.

Complete the captions 1

Complete the captions in the drawings below with a suitable idiom. Choose from the idioms using animals, colours or parts of the body in the last three exercises.

1 She's feeling _____ .

2 He's _____ to it.

3 He's taken _____ .

4 She's got _____ .

5 He's making _____
_____ .

6 She almost _____
_____ .

7 There's no _____
_____ .

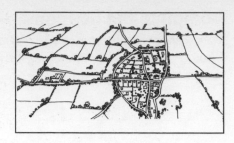

8 There's a_____
around this town.

9 She's a_____ .

10 He's giving him a_____
_____ .

11 It's a _____ party.

Five years ago   Now

12 He's gone _____ .

152

Read and discuss

Work in pairs or groups of three. Read through the following and take turns at answering. (The idioms are the ones on pages 145–150).

1 What sort of life do you lead if you **live from hand to mouth**?
2 Name three jobs that require that you use a lot of **grey matter**.
3 The new opera house has turned out to be a **white elephant**. It was built with Government money. Was it a good investment?
4 Try to make up a **cock-and-bull story** as to why you were late today.
5 He didn't take the job because he got **cold feet** at the last minute. What happened to him?
6 'I only said it **tongue-in-cheek**.' What did he mean?
7 Name four things that you do only **once in a blue moon**.
8 When was the last time you really **had a whale of a time**? Describe it.
9 He was **tickled pink** when he won the prize. How did he feel?
10 When you were a child did you ever **set your heart on something**? If so what, and did you get it?
11 She has just **got something off her chest**. How is she probably feeling?
12 Think up an example (a situation) of **killing two birds with one stone**.
13 Today was a **red-letter day** for her. Suggest why.
14 Name three things that might cause you to **have your heart in your mouth** while watching them.
15 'I won't believe it until I see it **in black and white**.' What does she mean?
16 He got it **straight from the horse's mouth**. Was the information reliable? Why or why not?
17 'I think I'll just go and **stretch my legs**.' What does this person want to do?
18 He **paid through the nose** for it. Did he get a bargain?

19 He **jumped down my throat**. Suggest why.

20 Name one or two things in your country that are difficult to come by or illegal but which are available on the **black market**.

Idioms using verbs 1

Fill in the missing idioms in the sentences below. Choose from the following and make any necessary changes, especially to verb endings and the words in italics.

bang *one's* head against a
   brick wall
bite off more than *one* can
   chew
blow *one's* own trumpet
carry the can
cost the earth
do wonders
drop a clanger
fly off the handle

get a move on
get *one's* fingers burnt
give *someone* the slip
go Dutch
hit the nail on the head
know *something* backwards
make a mountain out of a
   molehill
put two and two together

1 Tell Brian to _____, will you? The bus leaves in five minutes!

(Meaning: *Tell Brian to hurry up.*)

2 You really _____ when you said that Paul's problem was that he always wanted to be the centre of attention.

(Meaning: *You said exactly the right thing. You said something that was exactly right about Paul.*)

3 When the police discovered that the boyfriend of one of the cashiers at the bank was a well-known criminal, they _____ and began to suspect that the recent robbery there had been an inside job.

(Meaning: *They drew an obvious conclusion.*)

4 You really _____ telling her that the man in the corner was so boring. Didn't you realize it was her husband?
(Meaning: *You really made a mistake which caused embarrassment.*)

5 I hope you don't think I'm _____ when I say that I think I'm quite a good singer and really ought to be in the choir.
(Meaning: *I'm boasting; praising myself.*)

6 Joanna's been practising this piece of music for her piano exam next month. She's played it so often now that she _____.
(Meaning: *She knows it really well; she knows it thoroughly.*)

7 Have you seen Paula's engagement ring? All those diamonds! It must have _____!
(Meaning: *It must have been very expensive.*)

8 Charles will never vote Labour, so you're _____ trying to persuade him.
(Meaning: *You're trying to do something that is impossible; you'll have no chance with your efforts.*)

9 We only arrived five minutes late for the meeting, George! We didn't miss anything important really, so stop _____!
(Meaning: *Stop making something appear more important than it really is; stop exaggerating the importance of what happened.*)

10 The teacher really _____ when the students wouldn't stop talking during the test.
(Meaning: *The teacher lost his/her temper.*)

11 We shouldn't have agreed to deliver their order by the end of the month. I think we may have _____ this time.
(Meaning: *We may have agreed to do more than we're capable of doing.*)

12 I'm never going to buy shares again! The last time I invested in the stock market I _____ and lost most of my money.
(Meaning: *I suffered the consequences of an error of judgement; I had a bad experience.*)

13 One of the disadvantages of being a boss is that you have to _____ when things go wrong.

(Meaning: *You have to take the responsibility.*)

14 Since they were both students, whenever they went for a meal they always _____.

(Meaning: *They always shared the cost.*)

15 That self-hypnosis tape you lent me on giving up smoking has _____. I haven't felt like a cigarette for over two weeks.

(Meaning: *It has produced excellent results. It has had an astonishing effect.*)

16 After being chased by the police through the town centre, the teenage joy-riders finally managed to _____.

(Meaning: *They finally managed to escape from them.*)

Idioms using verbs 2

Fill in the missing idioms in the sentences below. Choose from the following and make any necessary changes, especially to verb endings and the words in italics.

bend over backwards	have a chip on *one's* shoulder
bite *someone's* head off	(not) hold water
blow *one's* top	make a go of
butter *someone* up	make a scene
come in handy	pull strings
get hold of the wrong end of the stick	put *one's* feet up
get into hot water	send *someone* to Coventry
give the game away	stand on *one's* own two feet

1 I always carry a penknife with me. You never know when it might _____.

(Meaning: *You never know when it might be useful.*)

2 John's _____ ever since he didn't get the promotion he was expecting.

(Meaning: *He's had a grievance; he's felt bitter and resentful.*)

3 You usually have to wait at least two years to be a member of this club, unless of course you know someone who can _____ for you.

(Meaning: *Someone who can use his or her influence.*)

4 You're twenty-five now Donald. It's time you _____ instead of expecting your mother and me to help you all the time.

(Meaning: *It's time you became independent and self-supporting; able to look after yourself without help.*)

5 Mr and Mrs Carter _____ to make their American guests feel at home.

(Meaning: *They tried very hard to please them.*)

6 Her arguments sounded good, but when you examined them carefully they didn't really _____.

(Meaning: *They weren't really logical; they didn't really make sense.*)

7 I'm really tired tonight. All I want to do is _____.

(Meaning: *All I want to do is sit down and rest; relax in a chair.*)

8 No, I didn't say that at all! As usual, you've _____!

(Meaning: *You've completely misunderstood.*)

9 Clive's workmates _____ because he had carried on working while they were on strike.

(Meaning: *They refused to speak to him.*)

10 The boss was in a bad mood today. She _____ just because I was five minutes late coming back from lunch.

(Meaning: *She spoke angrily to me; she reprimanded me.*)

11 She _____ with the team coach when she didn't turn up for the match until half time.

(Meaning: *She got into trouble.*)

12 I do hope Pam and Dave will _____ their new business. They deserve to succeed.

(Meaning: *I hope they will be successful.*)

13 Mum's going to _____ when she finds out that you've broken her favourite vase.

(Meaning: *She's going to become very angry; she's going to lose her temper.*)

14 It was supposed to be a surprise leaving-party for our boss, but his secretary _____ by asking him if his wife was coming to it.

(Meaning: *She unintentionally revealed a secret.*)

15 The couple next-door are always _____ in public. It's most embarrassing sometimes.

(Meaning: *They are always quarrelling loudly and violently.*)

16 Don't take any notice of him, Cathy. He's only trying to _____ so that you'll buy something off him.

(Meaning: *He's only trying to flatter you.*)

Idioms using verbs 3

Fill in the missing idioms in the sentences below. Choose from the following and make any necessary changes, especially to verb endings and the words in italics.

do the trick	put *one's* foot down
feel the pinch	run in the family
get wind of	take *someone* for a ride
have kittens	take (something) with a
hit the roof	pinch of salt
keep *one's* hand in	talk shop
let off steam	talk through *one's* hat
look daggers	tighten *one's* belt
(not) make head or tail of	

1 Mary _____ at the man who had let the door of the shop slam in her face.
(Meaning: *She looked angrily at him.*)

2 The children are all very artistic, just like their father and grandfather. It must _____.
(Meaning: *It must be a talent that is passed on from one generation to the next.*)

3 She says she's a book-keeping expert, but according to my brother, she's _____ and doesn't really know very much at all.
(Meaning: *She's talking nonsense.*)

4 The headteacher _____ when she caught the student cheating in the examination.
(Meaning: *She became very angry.*)

5 If I were you I'd _____ everything Harry says _____. He does tend to exaggerate a lot.
(Meaning: *Don't believe everything he says completely.*)

6 'Take this medicine three times a day,' the doctor said. 'It should _____ and cure your sore throat.'
(Meaning: *It should achieve the result you want; it should have the desired effect.*)

7 The man I bought my car from really _____. It turned out to be a stolen car!
(Meaning: *He deceived me; he tricked me; he cheated me.*)

8 He has just lost his job, so he is going to have to _____ until he finds a new one.
(Meaning: *He is going to have to live on less money; make economies; spend less money.*)

9 The police have _____ a plot to kidnap the Prime Minister during his visit to Northern Ireland.
(Meaning: *They have received early warning of something from a confidential source; they have received information secretly or by chance.*)

10 I hate going to a party with groups of doctors or nurses as they always seem to end up _____.

(Meaning: *They end up talking about their work*.)

11 Playing squash on Saturdays was my brother's way of _____.

(Meaning: *It was his way of getting rid of excess energy*.)

12 What with inflation and rising prices, most people nowadays are starting to _____.

(Meaning: *They are suffering from lack of money*.)

13 The mother decided to _____ and insist that her children kept their rooms tidy from now on.

(Meaning: *She insisted firmly*.)

14 My mother nearly _____ when I knocked over a very expensive table lamp. Fortunately my father managed to catch it before it hit the floor.

(Meaning: *My mother became very nervous and frightened; she was in a state of panic*.)

15 I've no idea what they're talking about. I can't _____ it. I just don't know the first thing about computers.

(Meaning: *I can't understand a word of it*.)

16 Although he no longer played the guitar professionally, he liked to _____ by playing occasionally at the local folk club.

(Meaning: *He liked to keep in practice; retain a skill*.)

Follow up

Rewrite the following sentences, replacing the words in italics with a suitable idiom. Choose from the ones on pages 154–160.

1 If we don't *hurry up* we'll miss the train!

2 You've *misunderstood everything* as usual! Why don't you listen properly?

3 I see Carol's *boasting* again. I've just heard her telling new members of the tennis club how good she is.

160

4 It was a very avant-garde film. To be honest, I couldn't *under-stand what it was all about.*

5 Because of the recession, many local shopkeepers are *suffering the effects of people having less money to spend.*

6 My parents *went to a lot of trouble* to make my new girlfriend feel welcome.

7 If things go wrong, then it's me and me alone who has to *take the responsibility.*

8 Don't do any business with him – he'll probably try to *cheat you.*

9 It was only when he went away to university that he started to *become independent and get by without help from others.*

10 I always keep a supply of candles at home – you never know when they might *be useful,* especially if there's a power cut.

11 She *made an embarrassing mistake* when she asked Mrs South how her husband was. She didn't know he had recently died.

12 I'm sorry, but that argument just doesn't *make sense.*

13 Don't listen to a word she says – she's *talking nonsense!*

14 It was a really boring party. Everyone there was *talking about their work.*

15 He *became very angry* when he saw two boys throwing stones at a cat.

Idioms of comparison using 'as' 1

Complete the idioms in the sentences on the next page with suitable nouns. Choose from the following:

chalk and cheese	a feather	lead	nails
a bat	a fiddle	life	a pancake
a cucumber	gold	mud	pie
ditchwater	a lark	mustard	a post

1 The sun was shining. The birds were singing. For the first time for ages, Philip felt as happy as _____.

2 He really enjoyed teaching them since they were all as keen as _____ to learn.

3 You'll have to speak up. Aunt Agatha is as deaf as _____.

4 'The bag isn't heavy, is it?'
   'No, it's as light as _____.'

5 His explanation was as clear as _____. I didn't understand a word of it!

6 It's hard to believe they're sisters as they're as different as _____.

7 She has always found learning foreign languages as easy as _____.

8 Although she was nearly fifty, she was still as fit as _____.

9 I'm sorry, I didn't recognize you, Paul, but I'm as blind as _____ without my glasses.

10 I was in the middle of Tokyo when who should I see – as large as _____ – none other than my cousin. What a surprise!

11 When the fire broke out, Gerald remained as cool as _____ and without panicking got everyone to safety before the fire brigade arrived.

12 We'll have to blow up this tyre – it's as flat as _____.

13 What have you got in this suitcase? It's as heavy as _____. I can hardly lift it.

14 The musical was a great disappointment. It was as dull as _____. I don't think I've ever seen such a boring production.

15 'How were the children?' the mother asked the baby-sitter. 'Oh, they've been as good as _____ all evening. Really marvellous.'

16 The new boss might look kind and sympathetic, but believe me, she's as hard as _____.

Idioms of comparison using 'as' 2

Complete the idioms in the sentences below with suitable nouns.
Choose from the following:

clockwork	the hills	leather	a rake
a dog	houses	a mouse	a sheet
a flash	a kitten	a mule	thieves
a hatter	a lamb	rain	toast

1 The meal at Philip's last night was dreadful! The meat was as tough as _____. It was almost impossible to cut and chew it.

2 Your money will be as safe as _____ if you invest in that company.

3 Although she wasn't feeling too well when she came home from school, by the morning she was as right as _____ again.

4 When they were students, Andy, Pete and Frank were as thick as _____ and went everywhere together.

5 Anne is very good at adding up figures. She's as quick as _____ and always works out the answers before I do, even though I'm using a calculator.

6 James ought to eat more. He's as thin as _____.

7 Do you like my new furry slippers? They're great, aren't they? My feet are as warm as _____ in them.

8 That's the last time I go fishing in the sea in a rowing boat. I was as sick as _____ the whole time.

9 You won't get her to change her mind, she's as stubborn as _____.

10 Don't listen to anything he says. Poor thing! He's as mad as _____.

11 I know my dog is big, but he won't bite you. Honestly, Mandy, he's as gentle as _____.

12 You carry on working, Pat. I won't disturb you. I promise to be as quiet as _____.

13 'Have you heard the joke about the camel and the undertaker?' 'Yes, we have. It's as old as _____.'

14 After the operation she felt as weak as _____ for weeks.

15 John suddenly put the phone down, his face as white as _____. 'It's my father. He's... he's dead!' he said in a trembling voice.

16 Mr Smith comes into my shop at eight-thirty to pick up the morning paper as regular as _____. You can almost set your watch by him.

Idioms of comparison using 'like'

Fill in the missing idioms in the sentences below. Choose from the following and make any necessary changes to the words in italics.

like the back of *one's* hand	like a light
like a bear with a sore head	like a log
like a bolt from the blue	like a red rag to a bull
like dirt	like a sieve
like a duck to water	like a sore thumb
like a fish out of water	like a ton of bricks
like a glove	like a Trojan
like hot cakes	like water off a duck's back
like a house on fire	like wildfire

1 When he left the army and went to work in a bank he felt _____ for the first few months.

(Meaning: *He felt out of place; unsuited for the work.*)

2 Mentioning Paul Rowley in front of Pauline is _____. She really hates him since he broke up with her sister.

(Meaning: *It is certain to make her angry.*)

3 I keep telling her to switch all the lights out when she goes to bed, but it's _____. She just doesn't take any notice.

(Meaning: *It has no effect at all; it makes no impression on her.*)

4 He has lived in Brighton all his life and knows it _____.

(Meaning: *He knows it really well; he is very familiar with the town.*)

5 From the moment my wife and I met, we got on _____.

(Meaning: *We enjoyed each other's company; we had a very good relationship.*)

6 If Mr Wilkins ever finds out that you cheated in the exam he'll come down on you _____.

(Meaning: *He'll punish you severely.*)

7 News of the assassination attempt spread _____.

(Meaning: *It spread very quickly.*)

8 The news of the Queen's death came _____.

(Meaning: *It came totally unexpectedly.*)

9 She was so tired after the long journey that she slept _____.

(Meaning: *She slept deeply and soundly.*)

10 She worked _____ all day to get the job finished.

(Meaning: *She worked very hard.*)

11 Something must have upset dad. He's been _____ all morning.

(Meaning: *He's been very irritable; he's been in a bad mood.*)

12 Although she had never used a word processor before getting the job, she took to it _____.

(Meaning: *She got used to it very quickly.*)

13 He was so tired that as soon as his head hit the pillow he went out _____ and didn't wake up until 10 o'clock the next morning.

(Meaning: *He fell asleep immediately.*)

14 Don't try for a job there. The pay is very low and they treat you
   _____.

   (Meaning: *They treat you very badly.*)

15 My grandfather never remembers any of our birthdays. He's got
   a memory _____.
   (Meaning: *He's got a very bad memory.*)

16 'Is the dress too small?'
   'No, it's perfect. It fits _____.'
   (Meaning: *It fits very well.*)

17 You can't build a modern office block in the middle of the Old
   Town. It will stick out _____!
   (Meaning: *It will be very conspicuous and out of place.*)

18 The new computer game was selling _____.
   (Meaning: *It was selling very quickly.*)

Complete the captions 2

Complete the captions in the drawings below with a suitable idiom.
Use an idiom of comparison from the ones on pages 161–166.

1 She's as_____.

2 He's as_____.

3 It fits like _____ .

4 They're as _____ .

5 They're as different as _____ _____ .

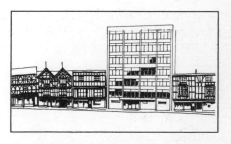

6 They got on like _____ _____ .

7 He's as _____ .

8 It sticks out like _____ _____ .

9 He's as _____ .

10 It's as _____ .

11 He's _____ .

12 He's gone as _____
_____ .

In other words...

(a) *Match the statements 1–10 with suitable idioms a–j. Write your*
answers in the boxes at the top of the next page.

1 'I've changed. I don't steal any more.'

2 'I've annoyed David in some way.'

3 'I keep telling him to give up smoking, but he won't listen.'

4 'I'm too frightened to drive these days.'

5 What a storm!

6 'I can't stop. I'm in a bit of a hurry!'

7 'I didn't like caviar when I first ate it, but I do now.'

8 He used the company's money to make himself rich.

9 'I love chocolates and cakes.'

10 John just doesn't have any tact.

a It's raining cats and dogs.

b He's got a sweet tooth.

c He's turned over a new leaf.

d He's pressed for time.

e It's like talking to a brick wall.

f He's like a bull in a china shop.

g He's rubbed him up the wrong way.

h It's an acquired taste.

i He's lost his nerve.

j He's been feathering his nest.

168

1	2	3	4	5	6	7	8	9	10

(b) *Now complete the following six dialogues with a suitable idiom. Choose from the above list and make any necessary changes.*

1 A: Shall we go over that report now, Pat?

  B: Some other time, Alan. I'm a bit _____ at the moment. Sorry! Must rush.

2 A: Do you like pickled herring?

  B: Well, I tried it once but didn't really take to it.

  A: No, I suppose it's _____. I didn't like it at first either, but I love it now.

3 A: Do you still go mountain-climbing?

  B: No, I've _____. Just the thought of climbing anything terrifies me now.

4 A: Another piece of cake, Rose?

  B: I shouldn't really. But you know me – I've always had _____.

5 A: Don't ask Ken to deal with customer complaints, whatever you do.

  B: Why not?

  A: He's _____. He's got no tact whatsoever. We'd get even more complaints I'm sure.

6 A: Do you think they'll play today?

  B: I doubt it. It's been _____ all morning. The ground must be soaking wet.

Check 2

This is a check to see how many words you can remember from Section Four, Section Five and Section Six. Try to do it without looking back at the previous pages.

1 By the way, I _____ that job after all. I couldn't face living abroad for three years.
   (a) broke off (b) turned down (c) handed in (d) fell through

2 I still can't believe he's dead. It's very hard to _____.
   (a) take in (b) get at (c) hold down (d) make out

3 We've _____ eggs, I'm afraid. Will you have a sausage instead?
   (a) grown out of (b) done away with (c) run out of
   (d) gone down with

4 I was trying to work but the continual noise of the traffic outside my window *put me off*. This means it _____.
   (a) distracted me (b) prevented me (c) annoyed me
   (d) delayed me

5 She put down the telephone while I was talking to her. She
   _____.
   (a) closed down (b) turned off (c) got away (d) hung up

6 She's out of work and receiving money from the government until she finds a new job. She's _____.
   (a) on the dole (b) at a loose end (c) down the drain
   (d) on her last legs.

7 He's good at gardening. He's got green _____.
   (a) hands (b) fingers (c) nails (d) legs

8 If you let the cat out of the bag, you _____.
   (a) get into trouble (b) talk about your problems
   (c) make an embarrassing mistake (d) reveal a secret

170

9 He was _____ after working hard all day.

   (a) browned-off   (b) hard up   (c) dead beat   (d) hot-headed

10 In this country, the Queen doesn't have any real power – she's just a _____.

   (a) general dogsbody   (b) scapegoat   (c) figurehead

   (d) jack-of-all-trades

11 He hasn't seen his sister for _____ years.

   (a) cat's   (b) donkey's   (c) monkey's   (d) dog's

12 Which person is surprised?

   (a) You could have knocked me down with a feather!

   (b) I got butterflies in my stomach!

   (c) I had my heart in my mouth!

   (d) I was like a cat on hot bricks!

13 Which man has lost his temper?

   (a) He barked up the wrong tree.

   (b) He jumped out of his skin.

   (c) He had kittens.

   (d) He flew off the handle.

14 She was very tired and slept like _____.

   (a) A Trojan   (b) a log   (c) a ton of bricks   (d) a post

15 He took me for a ride. He _____.

   (a) gave me a lift home   (b) teased me   (c) reprimanded me

   (d) tricked me

16 Read through the following sentences and try to work out what the missing words are. To help you, the first and last letters of the words are given.

   (a) We got soaked in a heavy d_____r on the way to the station.

   (b) It's strange how so many pop groups from the late seventies and early eighties are making a c_____k at the moment.

   (c) The factory has an annual t_____r of £3 million.

   (d) Despite an early s_____k, the project was completed on time.

(e) The o_____t of this disease is marked by a high temperature and vomiting.

(f) He's such a s_____t. He hates spending money and is really mean.

(g) He was called Robert but everyone knew him by his n_____e 'Piggy'.

(h) They were making such a r_____t in the flat above that he couldn't sleep.

(i) The government decision to put income tax up by 5 per cent is likely to cause a b_____h by angry voters.

(j) The cheque you send us every month is a g_____d. Without it, we wouldn't be able to manage.

(k) I love the hustle and b_____e of city life.

(l) For years they had to s_____p and save to make ends meet.

17 Match the words on the left with the words on the right. Draw lines between the correct pairs.

(a)

call on	increase (prices)
go down	investigate (something)
go in for	recover (from an accident or illness)
go off	visit (someone)
go up	go to bed
hold on	enter (a competition, an exam)
kick off	demolish, destroy (a building)
look into	sink (a ship)
pass away	wait
pull down	die
pull through	start (a game of football)
turn in	explode (a bomb)

(b)

at loggerheads	without any money
brainy	not well, ill
hair-raising	rich, wealthy
nosy	very happy
off colour	quarrelling
over the moon	frightening
pig-headed	mean (with money)
stony broke	inquisitive, curious
tight-fisted	intelligent
well-off	stubborn

(c)

as blind as	the hills
as cool as	rain
as fit as	a bat
as good as	a rake
as keen as	a cucumber
as old as	houses
as regular as	mustard
as right as	a fiddle
as safe as	clockwork
as thin as	gold

18 Say whether the following sentences are correct (C) or incorrect (I).

(a) If you don't **take to** a person, you don't really like him or her.

(b) They tried to defeat the government. They tried to **put** them **down**.

(c) You would probably feel very happy if you had a **windfall**.

(d) You don't usually try to **get out of** something you like doing.

(e) He felt **as weak as a mouse** after the operation.

(f) It was a wild guess. It was a **flash in the pan**.

(g) We didn't understand a word they said. It was all **double Dutch** to us.

(h) Most parents are happy when their children are **playing up**.

(i) Although they often quarrelled, they usually **made up** before they went to bed.

(j) There's nothing illegal or dishonest about the deal. It's all **above board**.

(k) I had put on weight, so I had to **tighten my belt**.

(l) They were talking about their work. They were **talking through their hats**.

19 Complete the following sentences using suitable prepositions.

(a) He got _____ hot water for not posting the letter.

(b) She was in a hurry, so she chose a book _____ random.

(c) He plays the piano _____ ear.

(d) Phone the fire brigade! My house is _____ fire!

(e) I learned to play the guitar _____ scratch.

(f) We'll have to use the stairs. The lift is _____ order.

(g) It was no accident. She did it _____ purpose.

(h) He left the country _____ good in 1984.

(i) The man was really funny and had us all _____ stitches.

(j) I didn't have time to prepare and had to answer _____ the top of my head.

(k) The people at this factory earn _____ average about £600 a week.

(l) The police arrived _____ the nick of time.

20 Rewrite the following sentences using suitable phrasal verbs. (Each phrasal verb should include the verb in brackets after the sentence.)

(a) I'm not very confident of passing the exam. (GET)
I don't think I'll _____

(b) When his aunt died he inherited a lot of money. (COME)
He _____

(c) He was too tired to stay awake. (DROP)
He was so _____

(d) We installed central heating only when we could afford it. (PUT)
We didn't _____

(e) How on earth could you disappoint them like that? (LET)
Whatever made you _____

(f) I can't wait for the holidays to start. (LOOK)
I'm really _____

21 Rewrite the following sentences using suitable idioms. (Each idiom should include the word in brackets after the sentence.)

(a) The flat cost a lot more money to buy than it was worth. (NOSE)
We had to _____

(b) 'You've misunderstood everything again,' she said to him. (STICK)
She told him _____

(c) It was difficult for them to live on the money they earned. (ENDS)
They had problems _____

(d) He has been in prison for three years. (BARS)
Three years ago he was _____

(e) We really enjoyed ourselves at the party. (WHALE)
We had _____

(f) I hardly ever go to the cinema. (MOON)
I only _____

(g) The only thing he thinks about is golf. (BRAIN)
He's got _____

(h) No one would speak to him because he had worked during the strike. (COVENTRY)
They _____

(i) 'Let's go for a short walk, shall we?' he suggested. (LEGS)
Why don't _____

(j) The station is very near the school. (STONE)
The school is only _____

(k) She is not very experienced. (EARS)
She is still _____

(l) We weren't sure whether he would get through the operation. (TOUCH)
It _____

(m) 'Let's meet at seven-thirty exactly'. (DOT)
They agreed _____

(n) We didn't hurry up, so we missed the train. (MOVE)
If _____

22 Complete the phrasal verbs in the following sentences.
(a) It was raining very heavily. It was _____ down.

(b) I met Cathy unexpectedly. I _____ into her in the High Street.

(c) We went with our visitors to the airport to _____ them off.

(d) This type of music has become very popular. It has really _____ on.

(e) _____ out! There's a car coming!

(f) I smoke fewer cigarettes now. I've _____ down.

(g) She imitated the boss. She _____ her off.

(h) Because she had bright red hair, she really _____ out in the group.

(i) They entered the house by force. They _____ in.

(j) In the end, he admitted that he had dropped the vase. He finally _____ up.

(k) She _____ on the dress to see if it was the right size.

(l) He let me stay the night at his flat. He _____ me up.

23 Complete the idioms in the following sentences.
   (a) After playing a game of rugby he was black _____.
   (b) She was an excellent speaker and had the gift _____.
   (c) Oh, what's the word? I know it! It's on _____.
   (d) My room is really small, there's no room _____.
   (e) The news of her death came like a bolt _____.
   (f) I only asked you a simple question. There's no need to jump _____.
   (g) You won't get him to change his mind. You're banging _____.
   (h) Although he saw what was happening, he turned _____ to it and pretended he hadn't noticed.

24 Find a suitable ending (a–j) for each of the following sentences (1–10). Write your answers in the boxes at the top of the next page.

   1 The room was so hot and stuffy

   2 He wasn't playing very well

   3 It was a formal dinner party

   4 They bought an old cottage cheaply

   5 She bought green curtains

   6 They made their getaway

   7 There was a very good turnout

   8 They spent a lot of money

   9 The recent outbreak of cholera

   10 The outcome of the talks

   a to go with her carpet.

   b on the upkeep of the house and gardens.

   c is not yet known.

   d that he almost passed out.

   e in a stolen car.

   f so he was left out of the team.

   g has claimed nearly two hundred lives.

   h so we dressed up for it.

   i for the meeting.

   j in order to do it up and sell it.

1	2	3	4	5	6	7	8	9	10

25 Here are eighteen idioms in alphabetical order. Write each idiom under the correct heading. (Three idioms under each.)

a blue-eyed boy
as quick as a flash
as thick as thieves
blow one's top
double Dutch
feather one's own nest
feel the pinch
get a move on
get on like a house on fire

have butterflies in one's stomach
hit the roof
in the red
like a bolt from the blue
like a cat on hot bricks
long-winded
see red
spread like wildfire
tongue-tied

friendship/liking someone
_____
_____
_____

anger
_____
_____
_____

anxiety/nervousness/suprise
_____
_____
_____

money/lack of money
_____
_____
_____

speech/silence
_____
_____
_____

speed
_____
_____
_____

26 Suggest answers to the following questions.
  (a) He's finally **settled down**. What's he done?
  (b) They wanted her to **stand down**. What did they want her to do?
  (c) They've been **laid off**. What's happened to them?
  (d) Why wouldn't you probably be happy if someone was **telling** you **off**?
  (e) She **sent on** my mail. What did she do?
  (f) It **comes out** next month. What could 'it' be?
  (g) They told her to **cheer up**. Why?
  (h) It took them two hours to **put** it **out**. What could 'it' be?
  (i) Where would you find a **by-pass**?
  (j) Who might you go to for a **check-up**?
  (k) How do you live if you **live from hand to mouth**?
  (l) It's two kilometres **as the crow flies**. What does this mean?
  (m) Who would be invited to a **hen party**?
  (n) Where would you expect to find a **green belt**?
  (o) He **made a pig of himself** at the party. What did he do?
  (p) Give an example of a **red-letter day**.
  (q) He **took to his heels**. What did he do?
  (r) She's **blowing her own trumpet** again. What is she doing?
  (s) Who pays for the meal at a restaurant when you **go Dutch**?
  (t) What do you do when you **turn over a new leaf**?

27 Complete the following crossword with the words that are missing from the sentences below.

Across →

4 It must cost the _____ to stay at that hotel.

7 He bent over _____ to make us all feel at home.

10 Don't mention the war when Uncle Albert is here. It's best to let _____ dogs lie.

11 It wasn't that important, James, so stop trying to make a _____ out of a molehill.

12 They say that caviar is an acquired _____.

14 We're all very musical. It runs in the _____.

16 Don't believe a word of it. It's another of his cock-and-_____ stories.

18 It's the right size. It fits like a _____.

19 I don't know how they could build that there. It sticks out like a _____ thumb!

20 We got up _____ and early to catch the train to London.

21 I don't know what's worrying you, Colin, but you'll feel much better if you talk to someone and get if off your _____.

22 All right! All right! Keep your _____ on!

25 I'm _____ and tired of learning English!

27 The exam was really easy. It was _____'s play.

28 He wasn't being serious. He said it all tongue-in-_____.

29 When the exams were over, the students decided to _____ the town red.

Down ↓

1 No, you can't do that! It's out of the _____!

2 Helen is always the life and _____ of the party.

3 If anything goes wrong, then Mary's the one who'll _____ the can.

5 I can't stop. I'm a bit _____ for time.

6 If you misbehave, he'll come down on you like a ton of _____.

8 They were very popular and sold like hot _____.

9 Since he was born in London he knew it like the back of his _____.

10 My cousin is the _____ image of the Prime Minister.

13 I didn't mean to say that. It was a slip of the _____.

14 He kept his _____ crossed that his son would pass his driving test.

15 I could never be a _____ and carry on working when everyone else is on strike.

16 Stop _____ about the bush. Just tell me to my face what the problem is.

17 The new boss and I got off on the wrong _____.

22 Take this penknife with you when you go camping. It might come in _____.

23 I always feel embarrassed when someone makes a _____ in a restaurant.

24 The thief managed to give the policeman the _____ by running into a busy underground railway station.

26 We decided to play a practical _____ on our teacher and put a FOR SALE sign on his car.

27 He had a _____ on his shoulder because he had never gone to university.

182

Answers

Section One: People

Types of people 1 (page 3)

1 – f	5 – a	9 – b	13 – i
2 – j	6 – l	10 – n	14 – c
3 – h	7 – m	11 – d	15 – e
4 – o	8 – g	12 – k	

Types of people 2 (page 4)

1 – d	5 – l	9 – b	13 – g
2 – k	6 – h	10 – o	14 – c
3 – f	7 – j	11 – e	15 – i
4 – a	8 – m	12 – n	

Type of people 3 (page 6)

5	an agnostic	12	a deserter	8	a snob	9	a veteran
10	a bully	4	a picket	2	a spendthrift	
14	a castaway	1	a proprietor	6	a sponger	
7	a conscientious objector	13	a sadist	11	a squatter	
		15	a scapegoat	3	a teetotaller	

Follow up (page 7)

1	genius	5	loner	10	sceptic	15	civilians
2	proprietor	6	charlatan	11	crank	
3	adjudicator	7	teetotaller	12	penfriend	
4	scrounger/ sponger	8	benefactor	13	nationalist	
		9	pickets	14	squatters	

Idioms to describe people (page 8)

1 – k	5 – m	9 – l	13 – c
2 – n	6 – a	10 – b	14 – h
3 – d	7 – o	11 – g	15 – j
4 – i	8 – e	12 – f	

Describing people: Character and personality 1 (page 10)

1 – f	6 – i	11 – s	16 – h
2 – l	7 – n	12 – d	17 – m
3 – p	8 – c	13 – q	18 – j
4 – t	9 – r	14 – b	19 – e
5 – a	10 – g	15 – k	20 – o

Describing people: Character and personality 2 (page 11)

1 – g	6 – t	11 – m	16 – r
2 – j	7 – o	12 – p	17 – f
3 – n	8 – a	13 – i	18 – l
4 – s	9 – q	14 – k	19 – c
5 – d	10 – e	15 – b	20 – h

Describing people: Character and personality 3 (page 13)

1 – k	6 – m	11 – p	16 – c
2 – o	7 – a	12 – s	17 – f
3 – g	8 – t	13 – b	18 – n
4 – q	9 – e	14 – r	19 – h
5 – i	10 – l	15 – j	20 – d

Describing people: Character and personality 4 (page 15)

7 bigoted	16 determined	5 indecisive	11 thrifty
4 blunt	1 extravagant	15 naïve	3 understanding
10 callous	12 fussy	2 possessive	13 unreliable
14 cynical	8 illiterate	9 superstitious	6 weak-willed

Describing people: Moods and feelings 1 (page 17)

1 – j	5 – p	9 – c	13 – b
2 – n	6 – a	10 – g	14 – k
3 – l	7 – i	11 – d	15 – e
4 – f	8 – o	12 – h	16 – m

Describing people: Moods and feelings 2 (page 19)

1 – f	5 – a	9 – b	13 – h
2 – i	6 – c	10 – g	14 – d
3 – l	7 – j	11 – n	15 – k
4 – o	8 – m	12 – e	

Follow up (page 20) *(Suggestions only. Other answers may be possible.)*

1 thrilled	5 petrified/scared	8 homesick	12 apprehensive
2 furious	6 disillusioned/	9 baffled	
3 amazed	fed up	10 touchy	
4 paranoid	7 heartbroken	11 nostalgic	

Jobs people do 1 (page 21)

1 – e	5 – a	9 – b	13 – c
2 – k	6 – d	10 – l	14 – i
3 – h	7 – j	11 – g	15 – f
4 – m	8 – n	12 – o	

Jobs people do 2 (page 23)

6 an archaeologist	5 a critic	4 a nanny	9 a taxidermist
3 a bodyguard	1 an editor	2 a solicitor	
7 a busker	8 a lifeguard	10 a surveyor	

Parts of the body (page 24)

1 *No key*

2

15	Adam's apple	6	lobe	23	armpit	18	knuckle
5	bags under the	11	mole	24	back	19	navel
	eyes	8	moustache	16	biceps	27	palm
4	crow's feet	7	nostril	25	bust	20	pot belly
10	dimple	1	parting	28	calf	21	shin
14	double chin	12	scar	17	fist		
2	eyelid	3	temple	26	hip		
9	freckles	13	wrinkles	22	instep		

Parts of the body verbs (page 27)

1	knuckle	4	toe	7	heading	10	nosing
2	stomach	5	elbowed	8	thumb	11	handed
3	foot	6	palm	9	face	12	shoulder

In other words... (page 28)

(a)

1 – f	4 – a	7 – d	10 – g
2 – j	5 – c	8 – b	
3 – h	6 – i	9 – e	

(b)

1	got the sack	3	keep a straight	4	had a soft spot	5	did if off the cuff
2	got it for a song		face		for	6	Give me your word

Section Two: Health and illness

Inside the body (page 30)

5	artery	4	heart	3	lung	11	skull
9	bladder	10	intestines	18	pelvis/hip-bone	17	spine/backbone
1	brain	8	kidney	14	ribs	6	vein
13	breastbone	19	kneecap	15	shin bone	20	vertebrae
12	collar bone	7	liver	16	shoulder blade	2	windpipe

Parts of the body idioms (page 32)

1 – e	5 – o	9 – a	13 – g
2 – j	6 – d	10 – c	14 – i
3 – h	7 – p	11 – m	15 – k
4 – l	8 – n	12 – b	16 – f

Follow up (page 35) *(Suggestion only.)*

1   The mother had a lump in her throat as she tried to talk about her dead son.
2   All right! all right! Calm down! There's no need to bite my head off!
3   He drove like a madman along the motorway and I had my heart in my mouth all the way to London.
4   I hope she doesn't bring her kid brother this time – he was a pain in the neck the last time he was here.

5   What have I done to Pamela? She's been giving me the cold shoulder all morning.
6   Seeing young people carrying racist banners really makes my blood boil.
7   She needs to eat more – she's all skin and bones.
8   She saw the girl taking sweets from the shop, but turned a blind eye.
9   When she found out that he hadn't done what he had promised to do, she really gave him a piece of her mind.
10 You're looking down in the mouth today, Terry. Come on, cheer up!

Medical equipment, etc. (page 34)

3	adhesive tape	19	(hypodermic)	11	sling	18	walking stick
10	bandage		needle	5	stethoscope	14	wheelchair
2	capsule	4	ointment	9	stretcher	6	X-ray
17	cotton wool	1	pill/tablet	16	thermometer		
7	crutch	15	plaster cast	12	tweezers		
13	hearing aid	20	safety pin	8	walking frame		

Who's who in medicine (page 36)

1 – e	6 – j	11 – f	16 – n
2 – i	7 – l	12 – b	17 – c
3 – m	8 – o	13 – q	18 – h
4 – p	9 – a	14 – g	19 – k
5 – s	10 – r	15 – t	20 – d

What's wrong with them? (page 38)

1	got a sore throat	6	got a temperature	12	got a black eye	18	got a stomach
2	broken his leg	7	caught a cold	13	sea-sick		ache
3	hard of hearing	8	pregnant	14	been stung	19	fainted
4	sprained her ankle	9	got a migraine	15	got a nose-bleed	20	got high blood-pressure
5	got a bad cough	10	blind	16	burnt himself		
		11	crippled	17	got a rash		

Common diseases, illnesses and conditions 1 (page 41)

1 – f	5 – j	9 – e	13 – i
2 – l	6 – d	10 – m	14 – k
3 – o	7 – a	11 – p	15 – c
4 – h	8 – n	12 – b	16 – g

Common diseases, illnesses and conditions 2 (page 43)

1 – i	5 – g	9 – d	13 – j
2 – l	6 – c	10 – m	14 – p
3 – e	7 – k	11 – a	15 – b
4 – o	8 – n	12 – h	16 – f

Follow up (page 45) (*Suggestion only.*)

1	a heart attack	3	measles	5	nausea	7	insomnia
2	fever	4	cramp	6	a coma	8	hay fever

Skin and body disorders (page 46)

4	a blister	1	a bump	2	a mole	3	a wart
8	a boil	10	a corn	9	pimples		
6	a bruise	7	a cut	5	varicose veins		

Group the words (page 47)

Medicine, medication and drugs
antibiotics
aspirin
cough mixture
insulin
laxative
lozenge
pain killler
sleeping tablet
tranquillizer
vaccination

Hospitals and accidents
ambulance
anaesthetic
emergency
fracture
kiss of life
operation
patient
unconscious
ward
X-ray

What's the difference?

1 An *antibiotic* is a medical substance, e.g. penicillin, that is produced by living things, and is able to stop the growth of harmful bacteria that have entered the body.
An *antiseptic* is a chemical substance that can kill bacteria and thus prevent disease in a wound.

2 A *sleeping tablet* is a pill or tablet that helps you to sleep.
A *tranquillizer* is a medicine or drug which calms the nerves and reduces tension.

3 A *fracture* is the cracking or breaking of a bone.
An *X-ray* is a picture of the inside of the body, for example, of a fracture.

4 A *vaccination* is an injection you are given to prevent you getting a certain disease, e.g. a vaccination against flu.
Anaesthetic is a substance you are given that stops you feeling pain, either in the whole of your body making you unconscious (general anaesthetic) or in a part of it when you are awake (local anaesthetic).

At the doctor's (page 48)

1	GP	5	receptionist	9	pulse	13	prescription
2	appointment	6	symptoms	10	blood pressure	14	medicine
3	surgery	7	couch	11	temperature	15	lung cancer
4	waiting-room	8	examination	12	stethoscope		

First aid (page 49)

Artificial respiration (The kiss of life)

The correct order is:
5 – 8 – 1 – 10 – 6 – 2 – 9 – 4 – 7 – 3

The full text is as follows:

Lie the casualty on his back and tilt back his head while supporting the back of his neck with the other hand. Keep the chin up and blow air deeply and slowly into either the mouth or the nose (sealing the other to prevent air escaping) until the chest rises, showing that you have inflated the lungs. If the chest fails to rise, check that you have the casualty's head in the correct position. If it still does not rise after this, check for an obstruction in the airway.

Remove your mouth and allow the air to escape from the lungs. Watch the chest fall. Repeat. If the heart is beating, the effect of the first few inflations should be a change in the casualty's colour from a blue-grey pallor towards pinkness. Give the first six to ten inflations fairly promptly, one after the other, then work according to the reaction of your casualty. If he is pinkish, he is probably getting enough oxygen so just keep going steadily. If he is still pale blue-grey, he is not getting an adequate supply of oxygen, so try to get more air into him quickly. But always wait for all the air to escape before you blow in again.

If the casualty begins to breathe again himself, let your inflations coincide with his own breathing in, and continue until you feel that he can cope alone. It can seem hopeless to go on with artificial respiration but persistence is sometimes rewarded even after as long as an hour, so keep going (as long as the heart is beating).

When the casualty is breathing naturally, place him in the recovery position and watch to make sure that breathing continues.

Treatment in various situations and emergencies (page 50)

5	an animal bite (not serious)	2	choking
8	bruising	11	cramp
12	burns	4	drowning
		10	feeling faint

6	headaches, migraine	9	poisoning
1	a heart attack	3	a stroke
7	a nose-bleed		

Follow up (page 52)

No set answers.

Useful verbs to do with health 1 (page 53)

1 – h	5 – n	9 – d	13 – p
2 – e	6 – c	10 – a	14 – i
3 – l	7 – j	11 – o	15 – b
4 – k	8 – m	12 – g	16 – f

Useful verbs to do with health 2 (page 54)

1	had a relapse	7	infected	13	fainted	19	maimed
2	recuperating	8	choked	14	blistered	20	healed
3	treating	9	X-ray	15	injured	21	disfigured
4	diagnosed	10	lost consciousness	16	vaccinate	22	contaminated
5	aching	11	disinfect	17	fractured	23	suffocate
6	suffered from	12	swelled up	18	bruised	24	sterilized

Other useful words to do with health (page 55)

1	infectious	6	blood transfusion	11	side-effects	17	invalid
2	operating theatre	7	intensive-care unit	12	epidemic	18	germs
3	post-mortem	8	quarantine	13	check-up	19	dose
4	sufferer	9	injection	14	plastic surgery	20	paralysis
5	alternative medicine	10	antidote	15	feverish		
				16	contagious		

In other words... (page 57)

(a)

1 – h	4 – a	7 – b	10 – f
2 – j	5 – g	8 – i	
3 – e	6 – d	9 – c	

(b)

1	pull your socks up	3	an early bird	5	made a bomb
2	on tenterhooks	4	under the weather	6	the spitting image

Section Three: Crime and punishment

Crimes and offences 1 (page 59)

1 – f	5 – k	9 – a	13 – e
2 – m	6 – c	10 – n	14 – b
3 – i	7 – l	11 – d	15 – j
4 – o	8 – g	12 – h	16 – p

Crimes and offences 2 (page 60)

1 – h	5 – p	9 – b	13 – o
2 – e	6 – a	10 – m	14 – l
3 – k	7 – j	11 – c	15 – i
4 – n	8 – f	12 – g	16 – d

Follow up (page 62)

1	embezzlement	4	arson	8	kidnapping
2	libel	5	manslaughter		(murder,
3	shoplifting	6	burglary		mugging,
	(pilfering)	7	smuggling		assault)

9 assassination
10 forgery

Criminals and wrongdoers (page 63)

1 – g	5 – p	9 – a	13 – b
2 – d	6 – j	10 – o	14 – f
3 – m	7 – l	11 – e	15 – k
4 – h	8 – n	12 – i	16 – c

More criminals and people to do with crime and wrongdoing (page 65)

1 – e	5 – h	9 – a	13 – f
2 – i	6 – k	10 – l	14 – c
3 – o	7 – d	11 – n	15 – j
4 – m	8 – p	12 – b	16 – g

Follow up (page 66)

1	FORGER	4	BURGLARY	7	SHOPLIFTER	9	ASSASSINA-TION
2	MURDER	5	KIDNAPPER	8	HOSTAGES		
3	THEFT	6	ROBBER			10	LIBEL

Idioms to do with crime (page 68)

(a)

1 – d	5 – h	9 – m	13 – b
2 – i	6 – c	10 – a	14 – g
3 – l	7 – k	11 – n	15 – e
4 – f	8 – o	12 – j	

(b) *(Suggestion only.)*

1	caught (the thieves) red-handed	6	did time
2	inside job	7	fallen off the back of a lorry
3	greased (a government official's) palm	8	got off scot-free
4	cooking the books	9	case a joint
5	go straight	10	did a bunk

Law and order: The police (page 70)

8	bullet-proof vest	12	magnifying glass	10	torch	5	walkie talkie
13	fingerprint	11	notebook	4	truncheon		
9	handcuffs	1	police officers	2	uniform		
3	helmet	7	riot shield	6	visor		

Law and order: In court (page 72)

1	Magistrates court	6	dock	13	prosecution	20	judge
2	Crown Court	7	witnesses	14	judge	21	sentence
3	Justice of the Peace	8	witness box	15	jury	22	acquitted
4	trial	9	oath	16	evidence	23	imprisonment
5	accused	10	testimony	17	guilty	24	fine
		11	barristers	18	guilty	25	put on probation
		12	defence	19	verdict		

The verdict is yours (page 73)

No key

Verbs to do with crime 1 (page 75)

1 – j	5 – h	9 – p	13 – k
2 – e	6 – l	10 – a	14 – b
3 – i	7 – c	11 – m	15 – g
4 – o	8 – n	12 – f	16 – d

Verbs to do with crime 2 (page 76)

1	robbed	7	imprisoned	13	sue	19	mugged
2	swindle	8	reprieved	14	burgle	20	prove
3	kidnapped	9	threatened	15	shoplifting	21	convicted
4	deported	10	blackmailed	16	assaulted	22	interrogated
5	trespassing	11	double-crossed	17	smuggling	23	defrauded
6	acquitted	12	pilfering	18	embezzled	24	prosecuted

Other useful words to do with crime (page 78)

1	internment	7	warrant	13	bail	19	custody
2	legislation	8	justice	14	loot	20	law-abiding
3	warder	9	amnesty	15	illicit	21	conviction
4	coroner...inquest	10	martial law	16	euthanasia	22	judicial
5	abolished	11	alibi	17	statement	23	on parole
6	injunction	12	damages	18	clues		

Sort out the texts (page 80)

The stories are as follows:

(1)

THE MOST CONSPICUOUS BREAK-IN ATTEMPT

A gang, determined to rob a Bermondsey tobacco warehouse, worked out that the best way of entry was through the roof. There was, however, the slight problem that it lay directly beneath an overhead railway line near London Bridge Station.

Undeterred, the gang dug out the gravel between the railway sleepers and filled it full of gelignite. They slightly overestimated the amount needed, and the resulting explosion closed three mainline stations for four hours, stranded thousands of commuters and brought rush-hour traffic to a complete standstill. The noise attracted police from a wide area, and the gang were forced to flee before they even had a chance to enter the building.

(2)

THE QUICKEST BANK ROBBERY DETECTION

When Eddie Blake slid a note to the cashier of a Nevada bank the message was clear. 'This is a hold-up,' it announced. 'Put all the money into a bag and hand it over.'

The girl did as she was asked and within minutes Blake was running through the crowded streets with his haul. An hour later, when he arrived breathlessly home, the police were waiting for him. His demand note had been written on the back of an envelope with his name and address on it.

In other words... (page 81)

(a)

1 – c	4 – i	7 – j	10 – f
2 – e	5 – a	8 – d	
3 – g	6 – h	9 – b	

(b)

1	rings a bell	3	my cup of tea	5	a piece of cake
2	bucketing down	4	all Greek to me	6	gets my goat

Check 1 (page 84)

1	(a) a hermit	4	(c) a picket	7	(d) conceited	10	(a) She's furious
2	(b) a veteran	5	(b) a chatterbox	8	(c) superstitious		
3	(d) a castaway	6	(a) gullible	9	(a) homesick		

11 (page 85) *(Suggestion only.)*

(a) spiteful *(All the other adjectives are positive ones.)*
(b) baffled *(All the other adjectives are to do with being frightened.)*
(c) thigh *(All the other words are parts of the face.)*
(d) truncheon *(All the other words are to do with medicine.)*
(e) busker *(All the other people work in a hospital or are something to do with healthcare.)*
(f) asthma *(You can catch all the other diseases.)*
(g) knuckle *(All the others are found inside the body.)*

12 (page 85)

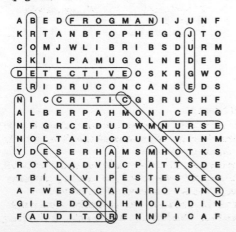

13   (page 86)

(a)   taxidermist   (d)   side effects   (g)   pregnant   (j)   plastic surgery
(b)   insomnia   (e)   optician's   (h)   tranquillizer   (k)   prescription
(c)   amputate   (f)   choked   (i)   dyslexia

14   (page 86)

assassination – political murder   kidnapping   – demand a ransom
arson   – set fire to buildings   manslaughter – death by accident
blackmail   – threaten to reveal a secret libel   – printing lies
burglary   – break into a house   perjury   – tell lies in court
fraud   – a false cheque   treason   – betray one's country

15   (page 87)

(a)   C   (g)   C
(b)   C   (h)   I (It was really cheap.)
(c)   I (An illiterate person cannot read or   (i)   C
      write.)   (j)   C
(d)   I (Crow's feet are the lines at the side of (k) I (He's the invigilator. The adjudicator
      the eyes.)   judges a contest.)
(e)   C   (l)   I (He's a lifeguard. A bodyguard
(f)   I (Bashful people are shy and usually   protects people's lives.)
      lack confidence.)

16   (page 87)

(a)   elbowed   (d)   hand
(b)   toe   (e)   foot
(c)   palm   (f)   stomach

17   (page 88)

(a)   broken his leg   (d)   sea-sick
(b)   got a rash   (e)   sprained her ankle
(c)   fainted

18   (page 89)

(a)   (b)

cure a disease   accuse someone of theft
deliver a baby   arrest someone for arson
dislocate a shoulder   ban someone from driving
dress a wound   charge someone with armed robbery
pull a muscle   take someone into custody
prescribe medicine   murder someone in cold blood

19   (pages 89 and 90)

(a)   crutch   (d)   stretcher   (g)   torch   (j)   magnifying glass
(b)   safety pin   (e)   tweezers   (h)   visor
(c)   stethoscope   (f)   handcuffs   (i)   helmet

20 (page 90) *(Suggestions only.)*

(a) ...really makes by blood boil.
(b) ...shaking like a leaf.
(c) I found it difficult to keep a straight face...
(d) I'm a bit under the weather/feeling under the weather today.
(e) ...is the spitting image of Andrew Lloyd-Webber?
(f) You've got to pull your socks up...
(g) He made a bomb...
(h) We greased the official's palm...
(i) ...was a piece of cake.
(j) That was a close shave...

21 (page 91)

Types of people	Adjectives to describe people (negative)	Adjectives to describe people (positive)
crank	callous	creative
genius	cheeky	enthusiastic
patriot	malicious	loyal
sadist	ruthless	sensible
sponger	two-faced	understanding

Criminals and wrongdoers	Diseases, illnesses and conditions	Crimes and offences
charlatan	amnesia	embezzlement
culprit	concussion	hijacking
imposter	cramp	perjury
traitor	indigestion	robbery
vandal	nausea	slander

22 (page 92)

(a) instep
(b) versatile
(c) civilian
(d) malnutrition
(e) wet blanket
(f) informer
(g) suffocate
(h) casualty
(i) amazed
(j) inquest
(k) contagious
(l) vandalism

23 (pages 93 and 94)

Across
3 hijacked 5 sprained 8 contaminated 10 face 11 serving 12 prove 13 pulling
16 aches 17 treat 18 broken 20 rob 21 kidnap 22 deported

Down
1 fractured 2 sterilize 4 convalesce 5 sue 6 diagnosed 7 vaccinated 8 committing
9 assaulting 14 imprisoned 15 healed 19 burgled

Section Four: Phrasal verbs

Phrasal verbs with 'down' (page 95)

(a)

1 pouring down
2 stand down
3 goes down
4 turn down
5 brings down
6 let (someone) down
7 run down
8 cut down
9 take down
10 hold down
11 pull down
12 closes down
13 play (something) down
14 gets (you) down
15 settle down
16 puts down

1	play down	6	settle down	11	went down	15	running
2	put (it) down	7	bring down	12	stand down		(people) down
3	took down	8	pouring down	13	pulled down		
4	getting (me) down	9	turned (it) down	14	cut down		
5	hold down	10	closes down	15	let (us) down		

Phrasal verbs with 'in' and 'into' (page 97)

(a)

1	hand in	6	talk (someone)	10	join into	15	comes in
2	run into		into	11	brings in	16	sinks in
3	turn in	7	look into	12	put in		
4	check in	8	come into	13	take in		
5	break in	9	turns into	14	fill in		

(b)

1	join in	5	checked in	9	turn in	13	come into
2	sunk in	6	ran into	10	look into	14	bring in
3	turned into	7	talk (me) into	11	came in	15	put in
4	fill in	8	broke in	12	take in	16	handed in

Phrasal verbs with 'off' (page 100)

(a)

1	kick off	6	pull (something)	10	wears off	15	drop off
2	see (someone) off		off	11	put (someone) off	16	show off
3	tell (someone) off	7	take off	12	keep off		
4	writes off	8	turn off	13	stop off		
5	break off	9	goes off	14	lays off		

(b)

1	put (him) off	6	taking off	11	dropped off	15	kicked off
2	stopped off	7	write (them) off	12	shows off	16	went off
3	turn off	8	broke off	13	wear off		
4	keep off	9	pull off	14	saw (our		
5	lay off	10	told (her) off		friends) off		

Complete the captions 1 (page 102)

1	dropped off	4	turned off	8	broken in	12	closed down
2	pouring down	5	come into	9	kicking off	13	showing off
3	checking in/	6	taking down	10	settled down	14	turned into
	checked in	7	seeing (her) off	11	joins in	15	pulling (it) down

Phrasal verbs with 'on' (page 104)

(a)

1	count on	5	drags on	9	catches on	13	call on
2	go on	6	brings on	10	pick on	14	live on
3	look on	7	hold on	11	try on	15	comes on
4	takes (you) on	8	turn on	12	getting on	16	send on

(b)

1	come on	5	brought on	9	call on	13	looked on
2	getting on	6	hold on	10	taking on	14	catch on
3	live on	7	send on	11	go on	15	drag on
4	try on	8	turn on	12	count on	16	pick on

Phrasal verbs with 'out' (page 107)

(a)

1	look out	5	breaks out	10	stands out	14	comes out
2	put out	6	dies out	11	leave (something) out	15	knocks out
3	try (something) out	7	turns out			16	runs out
		8	pass out	12	find out		
4	hand out	9	check out	13	make out		

(b)

1	find out	5	checking out	9	broke out	13	comes out
2	left out	6	knocked out	10	hand out	14	making out
3	pass out	7	runs out	11	stood out	15	die out
4	turns out	8	try (the car) out	12	Look out	16	put out

Phrasal verbs with 'up' (page 109)

(a)

1	hang up	6	blow (something) up	10	plays (you) up	15	pulls up
2	own up			11	comes up	16	go up
3	put (someone) up	7	make up	12	hold up		
4	grow up	8	slip up	13	cheer up		
5	sums up	9	do up	14	dress up		

(b)

1	dress up	5	cheer up	9	making up	13	hung up
2	held up	6	grow up	10	put (you) up	14	come up
3	pulled up	7	slipped up	11	do (it) up	15	gone up
4	summed up	8	blow up	12	owns up	16	playing up

Complete the captions 2 (page 111)

1	handing out	6	knocked (him) out	11	put (it) out	16	made up
2	passed out	7	trying (it) on	12	playing up	17	looking on
3	stands out	8	blown up	13	dragging on	18	checking out
4	catch on	9	gone up	14	hung up		
5	dressed up	10	Look out	15	run out		

Other useful phrasal verbs (page 114)

(a)

1	go through	5	get through	9	go over	14	go around/round
2	stand for	6	pulls through	10	take away	15	get away
3	take to	7	turn (someone) away	11	goes with	16	passed away
4	bring (someone) round	8	fall through	12	get at		
				13	takes over		

(b)

1	pull through	5	go with	10	get away
2	taken over	6	fell through	11	bring (her) round
3	go around/round	7	took to	12	passed away
4	turned (us) away	8	gone through	13	get at
		9	take away	14	stand for
				15	go over/go through
				16	get through

Three-part phrasal verbs 1 (page 116)

1 – d	4 – j	7 – k	10 – c
2 – i	5 – a	8 – b	11 – l
3 – g	6 – h	9 – e	12 – f

Three-part phrasal verbs 2 (page 117)

1 – e	4 – k	7 – h	10 – f
2 – i	5 – j	8 – d	11 – l
3 – g	6 – a	9 – b	12 – c

Nouns from phrasal verbs 1 (page 118)

1	hold-up	6	mix-up	11	take-off	16	kick-off
2	outcome	7	setback	12	flashback	17	by-pass
3	turnover	8	break-in	13	check-up	18	onset
4	breakdown	9	downpour	14	lay-by	19	handout
5	get-together	10	let-down	15	comeback	20	output

Nouns from phrasal verbs 2 (page 120)

1	outlook	6	break-up	11	cutbacks	16	follow-up
2	upkeep	7	layout	12	write-off	17	outbreak
3	intake	8	turnout	13	onlookers	18	knockout
4	drawbacks	9	breakthrough	14	come-down	19	stop-over
5	write-up	10	grown-ups	15	lookout	20	getaway

Follow up: Phrasal verb quiz (page 121)

(Suggestions only. Most answers are free answers.)

1 A business deal, house purchase, etc.
2 They weren't allowed into a building.
3 To the doctor, hospital, doctor's surgery, dentist.
4 The splitting of the atom, invention of the transistor, organ transplants, etc.
5 Free answer. *(Break-up of a marriage = ending of a marriage.)*
6 Free answer. *(Go with = match.)*
7 Free answer. *(Check up on someone = obtain information on them secretly.)*
8 Boxing.
9 Because it means she would recover *(after an illness or an accident.)*
10 National Aeronautics and Space Administration.
11 Free answer. *(Go down with = become ill with.)*
12 Free answer. *(Grow out of doing something = become too big or old to do or wear something.)*
13 It means it is so badly damaged, for example, after an accident that it isn't worth repairing.
14 Around a town.
15 Free answer. *(Look forward to = await something eagerly because you expect to enjoy it.)*
16 Because it means the friend had died.

17 Free answer. (*Make a comeback = become fashionable or popular again.*)
18 Free answer. (*Get round to doing = find the time to do something.*)
19 A play, a film, a book, etc.
20 Free answer. (*Drawbacks = disadvantages.*)
21 The police.
22 Pour water on their face, use smelling salts, etc.
23 Free answer. (*Live up to expectations = be as good as expected.*)
24 Free answer. (*Let-down = great disappointment.*)

In other words... (page 123)

(a)

1 – d	4 – a	7 – b	10 – c
2 – i	5 – h	8 – e	
3 – f	6 – j	9 – g	

(b)

1 green fingers	3 taken for a ride	5 black and blue	6 hold the fort
2 on the dole	4 make ends meet	all over	

Section Five: Idioms 1

Idioms using adjectives (page 125)

1	nosy	6	single-handed	11	tight-fisted	15	long-winded
2	thick-skinned	7	brainy	12	hard up ... stony	16	cheeky
3	well-off	8	tongue-tied		broke	17	hair-raising
4	browned-off	9	ill at ease	13	two-faced	18	pig-headed
5	hot-headed	10	down-at-heel	14	dog-eared	19	dead beat

Idioms using nouns (page 127)

1	loophole	6	backlash	11	nickname	16	bottleneck
2	scapegoat	7	brainwave	12	snag	17	godsend
3	windfall	8	skinflint	13	blow	18	catcall
4	figurehead	9	bloodbath	14	gimmick	19	heyday
5	hallmark	10	eye-opener	15	racket	20	nest egg

Idioms using adjectives and nouns (page 129)

1	short cut	6	practical joke	11	last straw	17	raw deal
2	sweeping	7	spitting image	12	double Dutch	18	mixed blessing
	statement	8	Wishful thinking	13	tight spot	19	dead heat
3	vicious circle	9	confirmed	14	sore point	20	red tape
4	golden handshake		bachelor	15	general dogsbody		
5	blue-eyed boy	10	stiff upper lip	16	tall order		

Idioms using noun phrases (page 131)

1	the life and soul of the party	7	a storm in a teacup	14	child's play
		8	a flash in the pan	15	the odd man out
2	A shot in the dark	9	a sight for sore eyes	16	elbow grease
3	a stick-in-the-mud	10	chicken-feed	17	the rat race
4	A fly in the ointment	11	teething troubles	18	a jack-of-all-trades
5	a blessing in disguise	12	a stone's throw	19	a drop in the ocean
6	the pros and cons	13	the gift of the gab	20	a slip of the tongue

Paired idioms (page 133)

1	games	6	square	11	touch	16	see
2	sound	7	later	12	choose	17	dried
3	wear	8	bustle	13	give	18	sick
4	downs	9	turn	14	scrimp	19	live
5	bright	10	change	15	buts	20	sweet

Complete the captions (page 135)

1	life and soul of the party	5	short cut	9	jack-of-all-trades
2	dead heat	6	odd man out	10	general dogsbody
3	gift of the gab	7	flash in the pan	11	sight for sore eyes
4	child's play	8	double Dutch	12	spitting image

Read and discuss (page 137)

Free answers.

Idioms using prepositions 1 (page 138)

1	in the flesh	7	up in arms	12	at random	19	for good
2	on the air	8	in a nutshell	13	out of tune	20	out of your
3	out of order	9	at a loose end	14	on fire		depth
4	by chance	10	on the tip of your	15	in deep water		
5	above board		tongue	16	on the house		
6	off the top of	11	in the nick of	17	in a flash		
	your head		time	18	behind bars		

Idioms using prepositions 2 (page 140)

1	on purpose	7	on his last legs	12	down the drain	18	in vain
2	over the moon	8	for the time being	13	on the dot	19	by ear
3	from scratch	9	at loggerheads	14	out of this world	20	in a rut
4	at short notice	10	on average	15	in stitches		
5	in the limelight	11	out of the	16	at will		
6	up my street		question	17	out of print		

Follow up (page 142)

1	in the flesh	5	on the dot	9	out of print
2	on purpose	6	at (such) short notice	10	in stitches
3	at a loose end	7	behind bars	11	at random
4	out of the question	8	on the house	12	out of my depth

In other words... (page 143)

(a)

1 – c	4 – a	7 – j	10 – d
2 – f	5 – h	8 – b	
3 – i	6 – e	9 – g	

(b)

1 off the beaten track
2 Get a move on... Keep your hair on
3 stop beating about the bush
4 you could have knocked me down with a feather
5 drop me a line
6 keep it under your hat

Section Six: Idioms 2

Idioms using animals (page 145)

1 killing two birds with one stone
2 put the cat among the pigeons
3 flogging a dead horse
4 make a pig of yourself
5 take the bull by the horns
6 get butterflies in your stomach
7 as the crow flies
8 no room to swing a cat
9 have a bee in your bonnet
10 cook someone's goose
11 smell a rat
12 hen party ... stag party
13 cock-and-bull story
14 straight from the horse's mouth
15 hold your horses
16 donkey's years
17 have a whale of a time
18 let sleeping dogs lie
19 gone to the dogs

Idioms using colours (page 147)

1 in the red
2 red-letter day
3 whitewash
4 black market
5 once in a blue moon
6 white-collar worker
7 give someone a black look
8 with flying colours
9 blackleg
10 red herring
11 white elephant
12 green belt
13 paint the town red
14 get the green light
15 see red
16 grey matter
17 green
18 tickled pink
19 in black and white
20 off colour

Idioms using parts of the body (page 149)

1 jump down someone's throat
2 set your heart on
3 wet behind the ears
4 get cold feet
5 lose your head
6 take to your heels
7 have your heart in your mouth
8 turn a blind eye to
9 get off on the wrong foot
10 live from hand to mouth
11 stick your neck out
12 jump out of your skin
13 tongue-in-cheek
14 keep your fingers crossed
15 get something off your chest
16 pay through the nose
17 have something on the brain
18 lose face
19 have your back to the wall
20 stretch your legs

Complete the captions 1 (page 151)

1 off colour
2 turning a blind eye
3 to his heels
4 butterflies in her stomach
5 a pig of himself
6 jumped out of her skin
7 room to swing a cat
8 green belt
9 blackleg
10 black look
11 hen
12 to the dogs

Read and discuss (page 153) *(Suggestions only. Mostly free answers.)*

1 A poor life where you spend money as soon as you earn it.
2 Free answer.
3 No. The building is expensive and useless.
4 Free answer.
5 He lost his nerve. He was afraid to take the job.
6 He wasn't being serious. It wasn't meant to be believed.
7 Free answer.
8 Free answer.
9 Very pleased, amused, etc.
10 Free answer.
11 Relieved.
12 Free answer.
13 Free answer.
14 Free answer.
15 She won't believe it until she sees it written down or in print.
16 Yes, probably. It came from a person who had close access to the information.
18 Go for a walk
19 No. He paid far more for it than it was worth
   Free answer.
20 Free answer.

Idioms using verbs 1 (page 154)

1 get a move on
2 hit the nail on the head
3 put two and two together
4 dropped a clanger
5 blowing my own trumpet
6 knows it backwards
7 cost the earth
8 banging your head against a brick wall
9 making a mountain out of a molehill
10 flew off the handle
11 bitten off more than we can chew
12 got my fingers burnt
13 carry the can
14 went Dutch
15 done wonders
16 give them the slip

Idioms using verbs 2 (page 156)

1 come in handy
2 had a chip on his shoulder
3 pull strings
4 stood on your own two feet
5 bent over backwards
6 hold water
7 put my feet up
8 got hold of the wrong end of the stick
9 sent him to Coventry
10 bit my head off
11 got into hot water
12 make a go of
13 blow her top
14 gave the game away
15 making a scene
16 butter you up

Idioms using verbs 3 (page 158)

1 looked daggers
2 run in the family
3 talking through her hat
4 hit the roof
5 take (everything Harry says) with a pinch of salt
6 do the trick
7 took me for a ride
8 tighten his belt
9 got wind of
10 talking shop
11 letting off steam
12 feel the pinch
13 put her foot down
14 had kittens
15 make head or tail of
16 keep his hand in

Follow up (page 160)

1 If we don't get a move on we'll miss the train!
2 You've got hold of the wrong end of the stick as usual...
3 I see Carol's blowing her own trumpet again...
4 It was a very avant-garde film. To be honest, I couldn't make head or tail of it.
5 Because of the recession, many local shopkeepers are feeling the pinch.
6 My parents bent over backwards to make my new girlfriend feel welcome.
7 If thing go wrong, then it's me and me alone who has to carry the can.
8 Don't do any business with him – he'll probably try to take you for a ride.

9   It was only when he went away to university that he started to stand on his own two feet.
'10 I always keep a supply of candles at home – you never know when they might come in handy, especially it there's a power cut.
11 She dropped a clanger when she asked Mrs South how her husband was...
12 I'm sorry, but that argument just doesn't hold water.
13 Don't listen to a word she says – she's talking through her hat!
14 It was a really boring party. Everyone there was talking shop.
15 He flew off the handle/blew his top/hit the roof when he saw two boys throwing stones at a cat.

Idioms of comparison using 'as' 1 (page 161)

1	a lark	5	mud	9	a bat	13	lead
2	mustard	6	chalk and cheese	10	life	14	ditchwater
3	a post	7	pie	11	a cucumber	15	gold
4	a feather	8	a fiddle	12	a pancake	16	nails

Idioms of comparison using 'as' 2 (page 163)

1	leather	5	a flash	9	a mule	13	the hills
2	houses	6	a rake	10	a hatter	14	a kitten
3	rain	7	toast	11	a lamb	15	a sheet
4	thieves	8	a dog	12	a mouse	16	clockwork

Idioms of comparison using 'like' (page 164)

1	like a fish out of water	7	like wildfire	13	like a light
2	like a red rag to a bull	8	like a bolt from the blue	14	like dirt
3	like water off a duck's back	9	like a log	15	like a sieve
4	like the back of his hand	10	like a Trojan	16	like a glove
5	like a house on fire	11	like a bear with a sore head	17	like a sore thumb
6	like a ton of bricks	13	like a duck to water	18	like hot cakes

Complete the captions 2 (page 166)

1	deaf as a post	4	fit as a fiddle	7	blind as a bat	10	flat as a pancake
2	thin as a rake	5	chalk and cheese	8	a sore thumb	11	sleeping like a log
3	a glove	6	a house on fire	9	gentle as a lamb	12	white as a sheet

In other words... (page 168)

(a)

1 – c		4 – i		7 – h		9 – b
2 – g		5 – a		8 – j		10 – f
3 – e		6 – d				

(b)

1	pressed for time	4	a sweet tooth	6	raining cats and dogs
2	an acquired taste	5	like a bull in a china shop		
3	lost my nerve				

Check 2 (page 170)

1 (b) turned down
2 (a) take in
3 (c) run out of
4 (a) distracted me
5 (d) hung up
6 (a) on the dole
7 (b) fingers
8 (d) reveal a secret
9 (c) dead beat
10 (c) figurehead
11 (b) donkey's
12 (a) You could have knocked me down with a feather!
13 (d) He flew off the handle.
14 (b) a log
15 (d) tricked me

16 (pages 171 and 172)

(a) downpour
(b) comeback
(c) turnover
(d) setback
(e) onset
(f) skinflint
(g) nickname
(h) racket
(i) backlash
(j) godsend
(k) bustle
(l) scrimp

17 (pages 172 and 173)

(a)

call on	visit (someone)
go down	sink (a ship)
go in for	enter (a competition, an exam)
go off	explode (a bomb)
go up	increase (prices)
hold on	wait
kick off	start (a game of football)
look into	investigate (something)
pass away	die
pull down	demolish, destroy (a building)
pull through	recover (from an accident or illness)
turn in	go to bed

(b)

at loggerheads	quarrelling
brainy	intelligent
hair-raising	frightening
nosy	inquisitive, curious
off colour	not well, ill
over the moon	very happy
pig-headed	stubborn
stony broke	without any money
tight-fisted	mean (with money)
well-off	rich, wealthy

(c)

as blind as a bat
as cool as a cucumber
as fit as a fiddle
as good as gold
as keen as mustard
as old as the hills
as regular as clockwork
as right as rain
as safe as houses
as thin as a rake

18 (pages 173 and 174)

(a) C
(b) I *(It should be they tried to bring them down.)*
(c) C *(It's an unexpected sum of money, for example from winning the Football Pools.)*
(d) C
(e) I *(It should be as weak as a kitten.)*
(f) I *(It should be a shot in the dark.)*
(g) C
(h) I *(They don't usually like their children misbehaving.)*
(i) C *(They became friends again.)*
(j) C
(k) I *(You tighten your belt when you try to spend less, to economize.)*
(l) I *(They were talking shop. To talk through your hat means to talk nonsense.)*

19 (page 174)

(a)	into	(d)	on	(g)	on	(j)	off
(b)	at	(e)	from	(h)	for	(k)	on
(c)	by	(f)	out of	(i)	in	(l)	in

20 (pages 174 and 175) *(Suggestions only.)*

(a) I don't think I'll get through the exam.
(b) He came into a lot of money when his aunt died.
(c) He was so tired that he dropped off.
(d) We didn't put in central heating until we could afford it.
(e) Whatever made you let them down like that?
(f) I'm really looking forward to the holidays.

21 (pages 175 and 176) *(Suggestions only.)*

(a) We had to pay through the nose for the flat.
(b) She told him (that) he had got hold of the wrong end of the stick again.
(c) They had problems making ends meet.
(d) Three years ago he was put behind bars.
(e) We had a whale of a time at the party.
(f) I only go to the cinema once in a blue moon.
(g) He's got golf on the brain.
(h) They sent him to Coventry because he had worked during the strike.
(i) Why don't we stretch our legs?
(j) The school is only a stone's throw from the station.
(k) She is still wet behind the ears.
(l) It was touch and go whether he would get through the operation.
(m) They agreed to meet at seven-thirty on the dot.
(n) If we had got a move on, we would have caught the train/we wouldn't have missed the train.

22 (page 176)

(a)	pouring/ bucketing	(d)	caught	(h)	stood	(l)	put
(b)	ran/bumped	(e)	Look	(i)	broke		
(c)	see	(f)	cut	(j)	owned		
		(g)	took	(k)	tried		

23 (page 177)

(a)	and blue all over	(d)	to swing a cat	(g)	your head against a brick wall
(b)	of the gab	(e)	from the blue		
(c)	the tip of my tongue	(f)	down my throat	(h)	a blind eye

24 (pages 177 and 178)

1 – d	4 – j 7 – i	9 – g	
2 – f	5 – a	8 – b	10 – c
3 – h	6 – e		

25 (page 178)

friendship/liking someone	**anger**	**anxiety/nervousness/ surprise**
a blue-eyed boy	blow one's top	have butterflies in one's stomach
as thick as thieves	hit the roof	like a bolt from the blue
get on like a house on fire	see red	like a cat on hot bricks

money/lack of money	Speech/silence	speed
feather one's own nest	double Dutch	as quick as a flash
feel the pinch	long-winded	get a move on
in the red	tongue-tied	spread like wildfire

26 (page 179) *(Suggestions only.)*

(a) He has got married, bought a house, started a family, etc.

(b) To resign or retire.

(c) They've lost their jobs.

(d) Because they were reprimanding you.

(e) She forwarded it to my new or present address.

(f) A new book.

(g) Because she was looking so miserable.

(h) A fire.

(i) Around a town or city.

(j) A doctor.

(k) In a poor way, spending any money you earn as soon as you get it.

(l) In a straight line – the shortest distance between the two points.

(m) Women only.

(n) Around a town or city.

(o) He ate and drank too much.

(p) Someone's fiftieth birthday, wedding day, etc.

(q) He ran away.

(r) She's boasting; she saying how good she is.

(s) You share the cost.

(t) You decide to change for the better.

27 (pages 180–182)

Across
4 earth   7 backwards   10 sleeping   11 mountain   12 taste   14 family   16 bull   18 glove
19 sore   20 bright   21 chest   22 hair   25 sick   27 child   28 cheek   29 paint

Down
1 question   2 soul   3 carry   5 pressed   6 bricks   8 cakes   9 hand   10 spitting
13 tongue   14 fingers   15 blackleg   16 beating   17 foot   22 handy   23 scene   24 slip
26 joke   27 chip

Key Words

The number after each word refers to the section in which the word appears.

get off scot-free 3
get on 4
get on for 4
get on like a house on fire 6
get one's fingers burnt 6
get one's goat 3
get out of 4
get (something) for a song 1
get (something) off one's chest 6
get the green light 6
get the sack 1
get through 4
get-together 4
get wind of 4
getaway 4
gift of the gab (the..) 5
gimmick 5
give and take 5
give (someone) a black look 6
give (someone) a piece of one's mind 2
give (someone) the cold shoulder 2
give (someone) the slip 6
give (someone) your word 1
give the game away 6
go (a)round 4
go back on 4
go back to 4
go bust 5
go down 4
go down with 4
go Dutch 6
go for a song 3
go in for 4
go off 4
go on 4
go out like a light 6
go over 4
go straight 3
go through 4
go through with 4
go to the dogs 6
go up 4
go with 4
godsend 5
golden handshake 5
GP (general practitioner) 2
grass widow 1

grease someone's palm 3
green (idiom) 6
green belt 6
grey matter 6
grow out of 4
grow up 4
grown-ups 4
guilty 3
guinea pig 1
gullible 1

hair-raising 5
hallmark 5
hand (verb) 1
hand in 4
hand out 4
handcuffs 3
handout 4
hang up 4
hard of hearing 2
hard up 5
have a bad cough 2
have a bee in one's bonnet 6
have a black eye 2
have a chip on one's shoulder 6
have a lump in one's throat 2
have a memory like a sieve 6
have a migraine 2
have a nose-bleed 2
have a rash 2
have a relapse 2
have a soft spot for (someone) 1
have a sore throat 2
have a stomach ache 2
have a sweet tooth 6
have a temperature 2
have a whale of a time 6
have green fingers 4
have high blood-pressure 2
have kittens 6
have one's back to the wall 2, 6
have one's heart in one's mouth 2, 6
have (something) on the brain 6
hay fever 2
head (verb) 1
headaches 2

headhunter 1
heal 2
hearing aid 2
heart 2
  heart attack 2
heartbroken 1
heel 1
helmet 3
hen party 6
hermit 1
heyday 5
highly-strung 1
hijack 3
hijacking 3
hip 1
hip-bone 2
hit and run 3
hit the nail on the head 6
hit the roof 6
hold down 4
hold on 4
hold the fort 4
hold up (a bank) 3
hold-up (noun) 4
hold water 6
hold your horses 6
home help 2
homesick 1
hospitable 1
hostage 3
hot-headed 5
humble 1
humiliated 1
hustle and bustle 5
(hypodermic) needle 2

ifs and buts 5
ill at ease 5
illicit 3
illiterate 1
impatient 1
imposter 1, 3
impressionable 1
imprison 3
imprisonment 3
in a flash 5
in a nutshell 5
in a rut 5
in black and white 6
in deep water 5
in stitches 5
in the flesh 5
in the limelight 5
in the nick of time 5
in the red 6

208

in vain 5
indecisive 1
indigestion 2
infant 1
infect 2
infectious 2
inflammation 2
influenza 2
informer 3
inject 2
injection 2
injunction 3
injure 2
inoculate 2
inquest 3
inside job 3
insomnia 2
instep 1
insulin 2
intake 4
intensive-care unit 2
internment 3
interrogate 3
intestines 2
invalid *(noun)* 2
invigilator 1
irritable 1

jack-of-all trades 5
jaw 1
join in 4
joy-riding 3
judge *(noun)* 3
judicial 3
jump down someone's
    throat 6
jump out of one's skin 6
junkie 3
jury 3
justice 3
Justice of the Peace *(JP)*
    3
juvenile 1
    juvenile delinquent 3

keep a straight face 1
keep off 4
keep one's fingers crossed
    6
keep one's hand in 6
keep *(something)* under
    one's hat 5
keep up with 4
keep your hair on! 5
kick-off *(noun)* 4

kick off *(verb)* 4
kidnap 3
kidnapping *(noun)* 3
kidney 2
kill two birds with one
    stone 6
kiss of life 2
knee 1
kneecap 2
knock out 4
knockout 4
know a place like the back
    of one's hand 6
know *(something)*
    backwards 6
knuckle *(noun)* 1
knuckle *(verb)* 1

lame duck 1
last straw 5
launder money 3
law-abiding 3
laxative 2
lay-by 4
lay off 4
layout 4
leave out 4
legislation 3
let-down *(noun)* 4
let down *(verb)* 4
let off steam 6
let sleeping dogs lie 6
let *(someone)* off 3
let the cat out of the bag
    4
level-headed 1
libel 3
life and soul of the party
    5
life imprisonment 3
lifeguard
light-headed 1
like a bear with a sore head
    6
like a bolt from the blue 6
like a bull in a china shop
    6
like a cat on hot bricks 4
like a fish out of water 6
like a red rag to a bull 6
like talking to a brick wall
    6
like water off a duck's back
    6
live and learn 5

live from hand to mouth
    6
live on 4
live up to 4
liver 2
lobe 1
locksmith 1
loner 1
long-winded 5
look daggers 6
look down on 4
look forward to 4
look into 4
look on 4
look out 4
lookout 4
loophole 5
loot *(noun)* 3
looting 3
lose consciousness 2
lose face 6
lose one's head 6
lose one's nerve 6
loyal 1
lozenge 2
lumberjack
lung 2
    lung cancer 2

Magistrates Court 3
magnifying glass 3
maim 2
make a bomb *(idiom)* 2
make a go of *(something)*
    6
make a mountain out of a
    molehill 6
make a pig of oneself 6
make a scene 6
make ends meet 4
(not) make head or tail of
    (something) 6
make one's blood boil 2
make out 4
make up *(verb)* 4
malaria 2
male nurse 2
malicious 1
malnutrition 2
manslaughter 3
martial law 3
matron 2
measles 2
medicine 2
midwife 2

surveyor   1
suspended sentence   3
sweeping statement   5
swell up   2
swindle   3
swindler   3
symptoms   2

tablet   2
take (something) with a
  pinch of salt   6
take away   4
take down   4
take in   4
take off (verb)   4
take-off (noun)   4
take on   4
take over   4
take (someone) for a ride
  6
take (someone) into custody
  3
take the bull by the horns
  6
take the mickey out of
  (someone)   1
take to   4
take to one's heels   6
take to (something) like a
  duck to water   6
take up on   4
taken for a ride   4
talented   1
talk (someone) into
  (something)   4
talk shop   6
talk through one's hat   6
tall order   5
taxidermist   1
teething troubles   5
teetotaller   1
tell (someone) off   4
temperature   2
temple (part of the body)
  1
terrorism   3
testimony   3
theft   3
thermometer   2
thick-skinned   5
thief   3

thigh   1
threaten   3
thrifty   1
thrilled   1
throat   1
thumb (noun)   1
thumb (verb)   1
tickled pink   6
tight-fisted   5
tight spot   5
tighten one's belt   6
toe (verb)   1
tomboy   1
tongue   1
  tongue-in-cheek   6
  tongue-tied   5
torch   3
toss and turn   5
touch and go   5
touchy   1
traitor   3
tranquillizer   2
transplant   2
treason·   3
treat (verb)   2
treat (someone) like dirt   6
trespass   3
trespassing (noun)   3
trial   3
truncheon   3
try a case   3
try on   4
try out   4
turn a blind eye to
  (something)   2, 6
turn away   4
turn down   4
turn in   4
turn into   4
turn off   4
turn on   4
turn out   4
turn over a new leaf   6
turnout   4
turnover   4
tweezers   2
twist (an ankle)   2
two-faced   1, 5
tycoon   1

unconscious   2

under the weather   2
underdog   1
understanding   1
underwriter   1
uniform   3
unreliable   1
up in arms   5
up someone's street   5
upkeep   4
ups and downs   5

vaccinate   2
vaccination   2
vandal   3
vandalism   3
vandalize   3
varicose veins   2
vein   2
verdict   3
versatile   1
vertebrae   2
veteran   1
vicious circle   5
victim   3
visor   3

waist   1
wait and see   5
waiting-room   2
walkie talkie   3
walking frame   2
walking stick   2
ward   2
warder   3
warrant   3
wart   2
weak-willed   1
wear and tear   5
wear off   4
welcome (someone) with
  open arms   2
well-mannered   1
well-off   5
wet behind the ears   6
wet blanket   1
wheelchair   2
white-collar worker   6
white elephant   6
whitewash (something)   6
windfall   5
windpipe   2